Conifers

HOW TO GROW
Conifers

Brian & Valerie Proudley

BLANDFORD PRESS
POOLE · DORSET

First published in the U.K. 1984 by Blandford Press, Link House, West Street, Poole, Dorset, BH15 1LL.

Copyright © 1984 Blandford Press Ltd.

Distributed in the United States by Sterling Publishing Co., Inc., 2 Park Avenue, New York, N.Y. 10016.

Adapted from material first published in GARDEN CONIFERS IN COLOUR.

British Library Cataloguing in Publication Data

Proudley, Brian
How to grow conifers.
1. Conifers
I. Title   II. Proudley, Valerie
635.9′775′2   SB437.5.C6

ISBN 0 7137 1426 3

Typeset in 9/11½pt Century Schoolbook by Poole Typesetting
Printed in Great Britain by R. J. Acford, Chichester, Sussex

Contents

Introduction 7

1 The Conifers and their Names 11

Plant names; Garden conifers

2 Conifers in the Garden 20

Framing the Garden; Continental gardens;
Rock and heather gardens; Ground cover and
foundation planting; Conifers in landscape design;
Background groups

3 Cultivation 33

Soil preparation; Position; Hedges and screens;
Specimens; Feeding; Planting; Containerised plants;
Reducing losses; Selecting quality plants

4 Problems 45

Transplanting; Physiological disorders;
Leaf scorch; Diseases; Insects

5 Growth Rate, Size and Shape 49

6 Descriptions of Useful Garden Conifers 52

Select Bibliography 90

Glossary 91

Index 93

Introduction

Most people, even if only remotely interested in the living world, should know what conifers are, for they are among the most frequently seen trees over almost all the temperate regions of the world. Each of the different kinds may not be known by name, but as a group many are known by sight by the obvious fact that most bear cones. This feature produced the title conifer: it is a compound Latin word derived from *conus*, 'a cone', and *fero*, 'bearing'. However, not all conifers have these cones. The seeds of junipers are found within a berry-like structure composed of tightly closed fleshy scales, and those of the yew, which has a hard nut-like seed, in a fleshy cupule. The old gardeners also called them 'balsams', on account of another property possessed by many conifers (and one which is still sometimes used as a guide to identity), the presence of sticky resin in buds, stems or foliage. This is also fallible, for other plants contain resin and, indeed, not all conifers have resin.

The first book in which conifers were described in some detail was *De Arboribus Coniferi*, written in Latin by the sixteenth-century naturalist Pierre Belon. When describing conifers, Belon had our common plants in mind, almost all of which are both cone-bearing and resinous in one way or another. These trees grew in his native France or nearby countries and were for many years the only 'conifers'. Botanists have since added many others, which as plants have major points in common. A typical wild conifer is characterised by its regular branch system and single trunk with the tree growing naturally into an upright, pyramidal form. As maturity approaches, many species lose their lower branches, leaving vigorous growth only at the top of the tree. In some trees, their style of growing is more bushy, with several stems or trunks springing from the base. They vary in stature from the completely prostrate *Juniperus procumbens* to the stately Coast redwood *(Sequoia sempervirens)* which attains 100m+ in Oregon, and holds the world record for the tallest tree. Another conifer closely related to that is *Sequoiadendron giganteum*, which is most probably the largest (and oldest) living organism ever to inhabit this planet.

The commercial value of the wood produced by conifers or softwoods (a misnomer, since many have extremely hard timber) is enormous. Large quantities are used annually in the building and furniture trades and also in the paper-making industry. (This page may originally have been part of a great Douglas fir growing in the Canadian Rocky Mountains.) The resin derived from conifers, when converted into turpentine by distillation, was formerly a vital part in the manufacture of paint and varnish. Although now largely replaced by synthetics, it still has its uses in some kinds of varnish and also medicine.

Garden conifers

Although different facts about the group may be fascinating, this book is primarily concerned with garden conifers which were originally developed from the wild species. Chapter 1 commences with the way in which they are classified in relation to other plants, and gives some of their origins. The second chapter deals with garden uses. Part of the advice passed on here was developed from an idea originally gleaned from Papworth's *Ornamental Gardening* published in London in 1823. In this book the landscaper is urged (and the same applies to someone gardening on a smaller scale) to think of the garden site as a bare canvas before the artist has gone to work on it. When completed, correct planting is the key to success in any garden, the canvas becoming more like a finished picture as the plants mature. Remember to construct features and plant so that there is always something to attract the eye whichever the season, be it high summer or mid-winter. Although almost every garden site is different with respect to soil, aspect and size, conifers come in such variety and form that permanent year-round interest is not difficult to provide. Having decided where to grow conifers, the next step is to discover how to grow them. Here we find that poor soil is no problem and where it is chalky there are many which thrive. We always advocate thorough preparation of the soil;

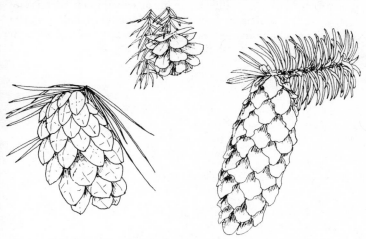

Three typical shapes of cone: *Pinus sylvestris* (left);
Tsuga heterophylla (centre); *Picea sitchensis* (right).

this is most important where conifers are to grow, for they have to remain in their one position for a very long time. Foresters seem so casual in their approach to this, yet seedlings planted by these experts seldom perish, but grow into fine forest trees with the (apparent) minimum of attention. Their method is to lift a spit of soil at one corner, take a small plant from a bag slung over the shoulder, drop it into the cut made, and finish the operation with a stamp from a heavy boot. Generally speaking, garden conifers require more care than this! For one thing, they are almost always larger than forest seedlings, and as they cost considerably more the risk of financial loss is greater if they die. Regarding cost, when purchased from a nursery good quality garden conifers can be expensive in terms of initial cash outlay. This should not deter anyone, for the money spent is small when you consider the many years of pleasure they will give. When it comes to the purchase of plants of any kind, wise shoppers are wary of cheap offers, for it is invariably a case of getting what you pay for, many so-called bargains often ending in disappointment. On the subject of costs it is also worth remembering that specimens take many seasons of skilled supervision before the nurseryman judges them fit for sale.

1
The Conifers and their Names

Although the differences between the various plant groups has been discerned for perhaps two thousand years or more even the greatest botanists struggled for centuries to find the key to the correct method of their classification. Today however all plant life is grouped according to the natural system developed by Engler (1892) and others who demonstrated that the plants' method of reproduction as well as other characteristics must be considered together. The flowering plants comprise of one of the thirteen great Divisions of the vegetable Kingdom. This in turn contains two Sub-divisions.

1 Angiospermae – in which the seeds are enclosed in a vessel or ovary. Here we find the grasses and 'true' flowering plants shrubs and trees.
2 Gymnospermae – in which the seeds are carried exposed on the scales of the female inflorescence.

The latter group is the one which interests us here for among its members is found the Class of Coniferae – the conifers.

In conifers the male and female flowers are always carried separately; in most genera they are on different pedicels on the same branch, in which case they are termed monoecious. Those with the two sexes on separate individuals are called dioecious. Examples of these are: ginkgo, Chile pine and yew. The gymnosperms, or naked seed plants, differ from the other flowering plants in that the unfertilised seeds are carried exposed on the female flower instead of being enclosed in an ovary or seed vessel. After fertilisation by wind-carried pollen, the scales on which the typical cone-bearing conifer seeds are carried become tightly shut within the cone until they are mature, or longer. This can take from six months to one, two, or more years according to species. When ripe, the cones open in dry weather in

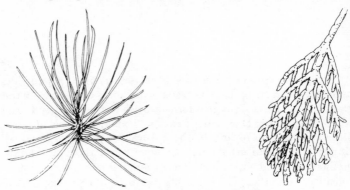

Two examples of the specialised foliage of coniferous trees: pine family (left); cypress family (right).

order that the winged seeds can drift away on the wind *(Pinus)*. Alternatively, the cones break up completely with seeds and scales falling together, leaving only the central 'fir candle' on the tree *(Abies)*. In the yew, the 'berries' get eaten by birds – by which means the indigestible hard kernels get carried off to sprout elsewhere. Conifer foliage is small, more often evergreen than deciduous. It can be needle and scale-like, as in the pines and spruces, or as in cypress and thuja with flattened angular leaves which overlap clasping the stem. The leathery leaves of *Araucaria* remain on the tree for ten years or more, yew and spruce leaves last for about five, whereas those of the pines can be anything from three to fifteen years old before they drop. Swamp cypress is one of the few deciduous conifers, and each autumn it loses both foliage and the small side-branchlets on which it was produced. The leaves of a conifer when raised from seed are at first unlike those of an adult tree, the plant passing through various stages before mature foliage is seen. After germination, the seed leaves, which can number from two to fifteen according to species, give way to juvenile foliage. Finally, the normal or adult leaves appear. Some species retain an intermediate stage in which both kinds are carried at the same time. Certain individual specimens in cultivation fail to assume the adult foliage form at all and remain entirely juvenile, even though the tree is years old.

Plant names

The early botanists had names for plants which could consist of one or several words, really a short description. This was cumbersome, to say the least, and général acceptance of a name sometimes depended on the personal stature of its author as much as anything else. It is to the eminent Swedish naturalist, Carl von Linné, more familiarly known as Linnaeus, that we are indebted for the binomial form of naming that we use today. Although not the first to use two words for a plant's name, he established this as standard practice for the reasoning behind it. So authoritative was his work to become that no name given to a plant prior to the year 1753, the date of the publication of the first edition of his *Species Plantarum*, is valid today unless it had been taken up by him for inclusion in the work, or by another author at a later date. Latin has always been the international language of natural science and is still used for descriptions of new species in botanical publications. As well as for species, Latin is also used for generic names and other divisions in the vegetable kingdom.

Families, genera and species

The scientific Latin name for the Scots pine is *Pinus sylvestris.* A closer look at the two words will tell us something of how the taxonomy, or correct botanical style, for an individual plant is arrived at. The name used as an example is that of a species: these are generally accepted to be a group of individuals, usually growing with others of the same appearance, whose progeny when raised from seed are virtually identical to their parent and bearing the same specific characters for generation after generation.

In addition to this, species often fall into a larger group termed a 'genus'; its members, although bearing a marked resemblance to one another, differ in some points. The next step up in the botanical arrangement is the plant 'family'. This consists of 'genera' (plural of genus) loosely banded together, but which again have similarities distinct enough to separate them from other such family groups. For example the generic name *Pinus* can be considered to belong to all the pines in general, but *sylvestris* is attached to a single species only. In other words, there are many pines, but only one species called *Pinus sylvestris* in the binomial system we use.

Supposing that someone in Japan wishes to describe a plant new to science, or a Russian botanist after much study decides that a species was originally placed in the incorrect genus, what do they do so that other workers throughout the world can be kept informed of their progress? In order to get the co-operation of all nationalities for a standard system of naming, the International Code of Botanical Nomenclature has evolved. Simple in theory (although not always in practice), an agreed set of rules always applies. One, known as the 'Rule of Priority', decrees that the earliest known combination of names is valid until such time that part of the name is subsequently altered as a result of further study.

In order to secure such a name the author, as he is termed, has to describe (in Latin) in a dated, recognised botanical publication the species he considers new to science, or, as happened in the past, show that he knows the details of and whereabouts of the original description or type specimen of the plant under review. Few new plants are found today, but often, as our hypothetical Russian taxonomist decides, a species was originally put in the wrong genus. When this has occurred one of two things can take place: the specific name can be linked to an existing genus; or if the plant is really distinct it can be used to start a genus of its own, sometimes taking other similar plants with it. A plant's specific name always remains with it, unless it results in a duplication of names.

Names are not changed lightly. Much research is undertaken before proposals of this sort are put forward and accepted by other botanists; and when it applies to the plants we grow in our gardens the name must also be accepted by the nurserymen, and finally gardeners themselves. So the quick answer to the question of who can name a species is anyone, providing that they keep to the established rules, although in practice it is the working botanists who undertake this sort of thing. In the case of conifers there are many synonyms which have come about as a result of changes. There are several instances of a name being used for some time before the discovery that it is antedated by another and, as the earliest name is the only valid name, the existing one has to be changed. Gardeners do not always take kindly to the revised title and so for this very reason obsolete names sometimes still appear in nursery lists. In books these names are often shown alongside the present name, together with the letters 'syn', to show that it was in former use.

Subspecies, varieties and forms

Although the species is the base on which botanical classification is founded, this is not the end of it. Certain plants do not fall neatly into the category in the simple sense of the word. When we spoke earlier of the species, we could have said that the progeny of each species is apparently identical to its parents. This is normally so, but as each seedling is a separate entity which comes about as a result of the union of the two sexes, minor

15

genetic changes can and do occur from time to time to cause a member to differ, perhaps very slightly, from its fellows. In most cases these changes are not noticeable, but once a change has taken place, after the passage of time, the altered plant may breed to produce a group much like itself. Sometimes more vigour is the result of the ability to withstand lower temperature. This may well have happened (after a great length of time), where a species is distributed over a wide range and a separate subspecies or geographical variant has taken the place of the 'type', as the original described form is termed. When growing together with the type, they are capable of freely interbreeding and of producing intermediates called 'interspecific hybrids', bearing features of both parents. Taxonomists formerly equated 'variety' or 'var.' (from the Latin *varietas)* with subspecies. Today the word 'subspecies' covers the distinct geographical races, and var. is used for a deviation from the type, individuals of which can occur mixed with it over much of its range. Although obviously belonging to the same species, these can have a distinct appearance where they are seen growing together. More difficult to classify when dealing with conifers is the word 'form'. This is adapted from the Latin *forma* and is used to describe a wild plant found growing with the type and in which some kind of change is apparent. Perhaps they will be low growing when an upright configuration is usual; some have glaucous leaves when green is typical. When brought into cultivation both vars and *forma* of the botanists can become the cultivars of the horticulturists. The word 'cultivar' is a recent term which is described later.

Hybrids

Another class of plants comes about when two genetically close species produce hybrid offspring after cross pollinating. Although rare, these interspecific hybrids are known in the wild and in cultivation. Another kind of hybrid comes about as the result of a cross between parents in different genera. These intergeneric hybrids are extremely rare, although the descendants of one of them are common. Hybrids between *Cupressus macrocarpa* and *Chamaecyparis nootkatensis* known as × *Cupressocyparis leylandii* come into this group. Each seedling is a separate clone which means that they can be perpetuated as a line of identical plants when propagated vegetatively. From the horticultural point of view, they are especially valued, for in combining traits from each parent their usefulness is extended. In this case one parent provided quick growth and tolerance of dry conditions; the other contributed thick foliage, hardiness and a preference for heavy soil, all adding up to one of the finest hedging and screening subjects that we have.

Garden conifers

A garden conifer can be a species, a subspecies, a *varietas* or *forma* or even a hybrid. The majority are, however, cultivars. Often written as 'cv' (or 'cvs' in the plural) this handy word is an abbreviated form of '*cultivated variety*' and is reserved for 'an assemblage of plants selected for some distinctive characteristic and remaining stable in cultivation'. Cultivars can be derived from wild plants – some are, but many more have originated in nurseries and gardens. Of those found several have appeared as mutants, genetically altered in form; some tiny when tall is normal *(Picea abies* 'Little Gem'), perhaps spreading instead of upright *(Sequoia sempervirens* 'Prostrata'), or with weeping branches in place of vertical *(Taxus baccata* 'Repandens'). Occasionally a stem bears foliage with cream or yellow variegation, together with the usual green. Once propagated by cuttings or grafting (in the case of conifers never from seed) they can retain their aberration to become useful subjects for the garden *(Juniperus chinensis* 'Variegata'). Seedlings differing from the original type in habit or colour or seedlings from existing cvs frequently appear in seedbeds, and these can also be a source of new plant material *(Chamaecyparis lawsoniana* 'Gnome').

Cultivar names

Briefly, horticulturists accept the botanical classification of the species adding to it the cultivar name. For an example we will look at *Thuja occidentalis* 'Rheingold'. As noted previously the Latin binominal printed in italics is the species to which the plant belongs. The cv name 'Rheingold' is always printed in Roman type, commences with a capital initial and is contained in single quotes. Since 1959 a cultivar name must be a 'fancy' one, i.e. not in Latin form. The advantage of printing in this manner is that the distinction is made clear at first glance. Who coins the names for new garden plants? As long as they consider the plant worthy enough, anyone can name a new garden plant after propagating it, but in so doing must choose a language other than Latin (which is reserved for species and their descriptions). Often in English, these names can be in any tongue capable of being printed in Roman type. As with the naming of species, there is a code of nomenclature which must be adhered to. Latin was much in vogue for the often descriptive 'fancy' names of conifers prior to the introduction of the code on 1 January 1954. These, such as *alpinus, nana, pygmaea* etc, when already given are still to be used but, again, printed in Roman and contained within single quotes ('Alpinus' etc).

Clones

Clone is a word linked to cultivar, for many of the man-made garden plants are also clones. It is a word used to describe a line of identical plants derived from a single original and as such each is part of, and therefore identical to, the 'mother', whether it was a seedling, mutant branch or sporting bud.

The value of using a single procedure and the Latin language for names and descriptions is immediately apparent when one considers that plant study and horticulture is international and has been for several hundred years. When it comes to garden plants, we have no reason to thank some of the early nurserymen for, in many instances, they have left behind a legacy of pseudo-botanical names, many of which almost defy the memory. It is difficult enough for the seasoned grower, but pity a beginner when confronted with a tiny pot-plant complete with a label three times as high as itself and bearing the legend: *Chamaecyparis pisifera* 'Plumosa Aurea Compacta'!

2
Conifers in the Garden

The fact that most conifers are evergreen immediately puts them high on the list of desirable garden plants, for their inclusion in any planting scheme gives an air of permanence which is lacking where only deciduous subjects are chosen. Even where the main floral display is from the often more colourful annual flowers, roses and shrubs, the conifers are valued as they act as a foil or backdrop for the rest of the planting, and by so doing complete the garden scene. It has been suggested that successful gardens have the same qualities as that of a good picture, namely colour, perspective, centre of interest and (by no means least) a good frame. Balance or scale comes into this too and it is only by the careful selection and placing of subjects that this can be achieved. The conifers described in these pages can provide, either alone or in company with other plants, all the components to create a garden 'as pretty as a picture'.

In developing this idea we will consider the main points in turn. Colour is something every garden needs. It seems there are some people who have the erroneous notion that conifers are just green things, the idea being based no doubt on recollections of old dusty specimens seen in towns and churchyards. This is bolstered by the fact that the majority of the conifers are evergreen. The word when applied to plants means that they retain their foliage for more than one season and are not necessarily *ever green*. Of course there are many in which green is the predominant colour, but this can be every conceivable shade, and few are dull. Most species have provided us with a glaucous grey or 'blue' form, others are yellow, gold or bronze often changing to a deeper tone in cold weather. Then there are those whose turn it is to delight us in the spring when their new growth emerges, brightly contrasting with the older foliage. Even in the green foliage plants there is often variegation where portions of the branchlets have a dappling of yellow and gold. Larger portions of the foliage are lacking in colour altogether and appear almost white in one or two sorts.

The deciduous species have their day when, at the end of the growing season, their leaves assume bright autumn shades before they fall at the onset of winter. From green to clear yellow for the ginkgo, others change to burnished gold or rusty-red before dropping. Several, particularly the taller evergreens, have a silver reverse to portions of each small leaf which is particularly noticeable when branches sway in a breeze.

So it can be seen that colour there most definitely is, and not too difficult to provide with a careful selection of types. Many conifers also have attractive bark, although the trees have to be nearly mature before this becomes really noticeable as garden colour. Anyone fortunate enough already to own any of these splendid older specimens will know the value of most of the pines for their decorative bark. Even the British native Scots pines are welcome for the bright orange bark they possess. The Wellingtonia has reddish orange bark up to an incredible 60 cm (2 ft) thick on a mature tree.

Framing the garden

Just as no picture is really complete without its frame, one could say that neither is a garden complete without its frame. The main difference is that in the case of a new garden the 'frame' (hedge or screen), unlike that of a painting, is often installed first in order to give protection to the young plants which are later to form the main part of the picture. The hedge has two purposes.

One, which has been mentioned above, is to protect the garden from wind. The other is as a screen to give privacy; to stop passers-by from peering in and to hide unsightly buildings etc from those looking out. The type of conifer to select for any purpose depends on a number of points, the most important of which is the scale of the mature planting in relation to its surrounds. This is especially so when plants for a hedge are chosen. The hybrid Leyland cypress are ideal when a quick

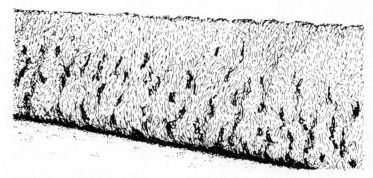

A mature conifer hedge can form an excellent protective windbreak.

growing, dense screen is needed, but an ultimate height of 3–4 m (about 12 ft) will be the minimum height to which they can be kept. For a lower finished height, several of the cvs of *Chamaecyparis lawsoniana, Ch. pisifera, Taxus* or *Thuja* will be better. When something really tall is required to protect the garden from severe wind then other factors have to be considered. Climate, soil and space available for development all have a bearing on what is to be grown. In mild seacoast areas, the ubiquitous Monterey cypress *(Cupressus macrocarpa)* or one of its close fellows are some of the best to have, for they withstand salt-laden winds well and are quick in growth. Young plants are not always prepared to stand up to the worst of the elements, but when given a little protection in the form of other evergreen branches, or hessian stretched on stakes, they will quickly establish and very few will be lost from bad weather.

Several of the pines grow to form a dense natural barrier, and there are species suitable for almost any soil or situation. Some pines grow well in cold areas, and here too the Norway spruce is at home. The best plants are not those grown from 'Christmas trees' but selected forest seedlings with a good fibrous root system. For screening in cold, inclement places, you should also consider *Chamaecyparis nootkatensis* from Alaska and its hybrid offspring Leyland cypress. *Tsuga heterophylla*, the Western hemlock spruce, grows better when there is no lime present in the soil, and as well as forming a dense, graceful screen withstands clipping into a hedge surprisingly well. Another hedge plant for cold parts is *Thuja occidentalis*, which is hardier than its other North American ally, the Western red cedar. Except when planting a hedge, the subjects chosen for screening are better when set in several staggered rows in order that they can establish a wind-resisting barrier and give mutual protection more quickly. Plant thickly and thin as development takes place over the years.

Continental gardens

When driving through France we once saw a most attractive garden layout in which conifers played the main role. In flat country, the site was obviously very windy with little to stop the sea gales from tearing ordinary things to pieces. A mixture of a compact form of Austrian pine and various spruces surrounded the house on three sides with the fourth left more or less open to the sun. Around the outside of the screen were more dwarf pines and the clear blue of *Picea pungens* forms stood out clearly. Junipers both upright and prostrate were sited near the building to provide a change in colour and form. Here were also planted drifts of evergreen azaleas for bright spring colour, plants impossible to have unless protected from wind. In addition to protection from cold winds, conifers are also used extensively, particularly in hot climates, to shade the house and garden from the sun. There are many desirable residences in southern Spain set amidst the umbrella pines and other species for this reason. Here too are the dark spires of the fastigiate Italian cypress, *Cupressus sempervirens* 'Stricta', the colourful blue *Cupressus glabra* and another cypress *C. lusitanica* which originated in Mexico. Protection from sun, as well as garden beautification, is an important use for conifers in other warm climates as well. In Australasia, they compete with gum trees for this purpose and in California, too, many conifers can be seen.

Rock and heather gardens

One of the more interesting uses for conifers is that of their place as feature plants in a rock garden or heather bed. Suitable sorts blend very well with other planting in positions such as these. No heather garden is really complete without its selection of slow-growing conifers which are needed to break the flatness of the low mounded heathers.

For preference do not use any but upright forms with a moderate speed of growth unless elite specimens of miniatures can be obtained. *Thuja* 'Rheingold', *Chamaecyparis* 'Boulevard' and *Juniperus communis* 'Hibernica' and similar are the ones to choose. Prostrate or extremely slow types are better on the rock garden or bed of their own; planted with the heathers they are liable to get swamped. The heather garden is one of the few instances when solitary specimens look right, even when spaced well apart. Generally speaking, conifers not only look better when planted *en masse,* or at least in groups, but seem to grow better with others for company.

On the rock garden some kinds can go in singly, others in groups. For example, where space permits there are few nicer

24

sights in a garden than a small gathering of the Noah's Ark tree *Juniperus communis* 'Compressa', each of varying height planted in a scree or pebble garden and accompanied by, perhaps, kabscia saxifrages or other choice plants and tiny bulbs. The bright green cones of *Picea glauca* 'Conica', looking as prim as if they had just been clipped, will also command much attention when grouped together rather than spread out around the garden. They can be put to one side of the main rock work but at ground level so that their eventual height does not detract the eye from the main rock feature. Be most careful to see that they do not form a row when seen from different angles, for, as Capability Brown the great landscape improver once rightly said, 'nature abhors a straight line'. Also refuse the temptation

How to use conifers to add interest to a rock garden.

to place an upright grower at the topmost point of the rocks. Here may seem just the place for an 'Ellwoodii' or similar, put there to emphasise the height of the rockwork, but a more natural effect is to be gained by copying nature instead. In a similar situation in the wild, the upright growers are not found on the summit but sheltering in the valleys or beside rocks. We can create a natural effect by putting them on the level where they will furnish the foreground. For near the summit the more procumbent growers look right while the rounded shapes of the dwarf pines belong where they provide height without dominating the scene.

One of the more important aspects regarding the choice of suitable companions for the naturally dwarf conifers is to see that once developed they are all on a suitable similar scale. Tiny pots of alpine plants and young heathers planted at the same time as alpine conifers can so often give the wrong impression when first acquired. It may not be too long before 'alpines' and strong heathers overpower the little trees in a takeover bid for the ground space. Grouped together in a special bed of their own is about the best way of displaying a collection of these gems. Their varied shapes and colouring can give increasing pleasure as they slowly attain maturity. Really these are a fine investment, one of the best as far as gardening goes, for once planted they require the minimum of upkeep and go on improving in appearance year in year out.

These are plants which can be placed fairly closely to start off with and then spaced out as time goes by. Moved on regularly, most transplant with ease.

Ground cover and foundation planting

We read a lot about ground cover these days and all the advantages in reduced garden work when weeds are smothered. Provided that the soil has been well prepared, with all perennial weeds removed, there are certain types of conifers which can be utilised for ground cover, and an excellent job they make of it too.

Select from the prostrate growers such as *Juniperus horizontalis* cvs, *J. sabina* 'Tamariscifolia' and the low forms of *J. communis*. Then there are the rapid growing Pfitzers junipers where a little more height does not matter. Low growing yews and their allies can take the place of the junipers if the ground to be covered is in the shade. Another use for carpeters is on graves which need to go for long periods without maintenance; here only the smallest of the prostrate cvs will suffice.

Foundation planting is the term used in some countries including the United States for the shrubs that are used to cover up and hide the foundations of new houses. Unlike in Britain where a different system of building is employed, the ground floor level is at some height from the ground. Here, quick-growing, dense bushy shrubs have to be employed to take away the bareness of the new walls. There are few finer subjects for this job than the many cvs of Juniperus 'Pfitzerana'. Left to their own devices many can get too large in time, even in Britain, but fortunately they respond well to pruning, and whole branches can be removed if needed. When tackling this job, lift the branches up and cut in a spot well out of sight making sure that there are no snags left jutting out to injure anyone passing by closely in the dark. Even where foundations do not require to be hidden, conifers can still play their role in furnishing the bare soil at the base of a house wall.

Very often there is a border left immediately adjacent to a building. This is frequently planted with bedding-out plants which are sometimes satisfactory and sometimes not. If this area were to be used to accommodate a selection of slow-growing conifers, not only would the need for annual replacements be done away with but, as permanent subjects, the conifers would provide year-round interest. While near the house, it should be mentioned that a matching pair of slender conifers is often used to make an imposing frame to the main entrance door. The dark green columns of the Florence Court or Irish yew, *Taxus baccata* 'Fastigiata', can look splendid in this position. Sometimes two specimens of a cv of Lawson cypress are used instead. 'Fletcheri' would be a good choice for this position and would not need trimming to keep their dense conical shape. In the Netherlands we have seen *Juniperus* 'Skyrocket' planted right against a

27

house wall, the blue-grey foliage rising spire-like to the first-floor eaves, to relieve the monotone of the yellow brick.

Do not forget that conifers grow well in tubs. These can accommodate smaller Lawsons, 'Ellwoodii' or 'Ellwood's Gold'; *Thuja* 'Rheingold' and *Chamaecyparis* 'Boulevard' are others which can be placed on the patio near the house to make an attractive feature.

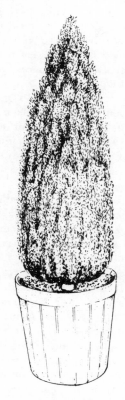

Conifers lend themselves well to being grown in a tub as decoration.

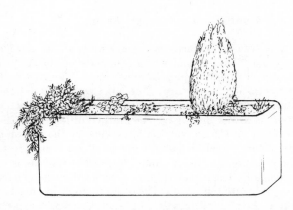

Small-growing conifers give a look of maturity to a trough garden.

Trough gardens are also better when displayed near the house for as well as being on hand to be admired they can get the watering needed in dry weather. They always require the addition of a conifer or two in order to create an established look. Only mini-size growers are wanted here, of course, and once again the tiny *Juniperus communis* 'Compressa' is the favourite and first choice for most. *Thuja plicata* 'Rogersii' with its golden foliage tipped with orange is another little plant which tolerates the restrictions of a trough garden for many years. These two and other small growers will be a useful addition to the alpine house, providing decoration when late summer and winter flowers are scarce. Bright blue when grown out of doors, 'Boulevard' is even better under glass and can cope with life in a large pot for many seasons.

The tiny growers take on a different personality when viewed from close at hand. The term 'living works of art' is usually reserved for bonsai, but it could equally apply to these little gems. Should they at any time get too large for their position just pop them into the garden.

Conifers in landscape design

Earlier we wrote of the similarity between a well planned garden and a good picture. The parallel is now continued on the subject of overall design. The landscape painter has three areas to bear in mind when composing his picture. These are the foreground, the middle distance and the background. The planter has exactly the same places to consider but with some marked differences. The artist puts down on the canvas his ideal view of the matured scene (either entirely real or part imagination) when seen from one position at a single point in time. The gardener's task is to attempt to visualise the mature planting as it will develop over the years – a very different thing. The other main difference lies in the fact that the painter puts down on canvas a single aspect. The gardener, on the other hand, has to consider vistas from several different approaches. In this respect he comes nearer the art of the sculptor who places his creation where it can be appreciated from different angles.

We have already seen how conifers can be used to form a 'frame' for the garden and at the same time protect the plants within. To use the word in a different sense provides the key to another valuable use for them – that of framing other planting. In Britain this is what is meant by 'foundation planting'. The successful planter uses vertical conifers in the foreground to frame the distant parts.

In former days, when great estates were laid out in a grand manner, the largest growing species were used with good effect although they are probably only now maturing the way the landscaper visualised them. Graceful cedars were placed on the lawn near the house, Swamp cypress by the lake and mighty Wellingtonias in the distance. Today, few people will be planting in this way although the same principles apply. Put some evergreen trees close at hand to accentuate the depth of the site with specimens placed strategically where they create a focal point and give perspective. The latter are rather like living statues and the choicest species should be selected for them.

When it comes to choosing specimens it is important to see that they will not get too large in relation to other nearby subjects. So, if a large grower is wanted try to give it an area to itself to prevent this happening. Few people today when planting for effect will be thinking of their great-grandchildren; they want to see results from the outset. Thinking along these lines we would not hesitate to plant a cedar which will give great pleasure for many years, although it will eventually outgrow its position and need to be felled. If it can be arranged that other plants can go instead, then so much the better, for it is the hardest decision in the world to have to condemn one of these noble trees to the axe before it has reached its prime. Not all trees that have outgrown their place get removed, for we have all seen those favourites of the Victorian gardener, the Monkey-puzzle, *Araucaria araucana*, dominating both house and garden. They seem so out of place to us especially when sited in suburban front gardens as so many thousands were. Most have now gone but for the occasional one hundred year old specimen towering above all. How surprised the planter who bore home the tiny potted seedling would be if he could see his coveted possession now!

Background groups

For a background, conifers in scale with the rest of the garden are ideal, but do be careful to see that they do not get so large as to be dominant. The whole effect of a garden feature can be lost if the eye is carried past and out towards the boundary. By placing a small group of conifers at a suitable distance from the house this can itself form a background for a feature such as a heather bed or rockery. The eye is then drawn down to this and attention is focused on the centre of interest.

Once established these carefully sited specimens tend to hide other parts of the garden from view and as all is not seen at first glance this adds a sense of mystery. This is an asset making the viewer want to find out 'what is around the corner'. On reaching the point from where the view was formerly obscured another and this time totally different vista is opened up.

These then are some ideas for the picture; it now remains for the artist to carry out the work.

Conifers used in background groups can highlight other garden features.

3
Cultivation

Conifers are, with a few exceptions, tolerant of a wide range of soil types, both heavy (containing clay) and light (sandy). The shallow chalk soils which contain much free lime are the exception, although there are suitable species which thrive even here. Many of the junipers seem actually to grow better when lime is present in the soil. If pines are wanted then there are *P. mugo*, *P. sylvestris* and *P. nigra* as well as others which will be satisfactory. *Taxus*, *Thuja* and its near relative *Thujopsis* are also content in a limy soil.

From this it can be seen that although the number of species is somewhat limited there is enough variation in these few to fulfil the average needs for hedging, screening, rock garden, winter-flowering heather bed and as isolated specimens. Except for the Swamp cypress *Taxodium*, no conifers are really satisfactory in a very wet soil or where water remains stagnant for long periods. *Tsuga* sp, the graceful Dawn cypress, *Metasequoia*, *Sciadopitys*, most of the spruces and Silver firs thrive in a *free-draining* damp soil. Where there is high rainfall as well as damp soil Sitka spruce, *Picea sitchensis*, is the foresters' choice and gardeners too should find this plant of value where a quick grower is needed. From wet places we now turn to the other extreme – that of dry, sandy soil. Almost all the pines will flourish here and there are also the junipers and cypress which all tolerate dry conditions well.

Soil preparation

All soil types will benefit from the addition of plenty of humus. This can be in the form of peat, compost, *old* manure, leaf-mould or debris from the forest floor. All these materials help to condition the soil, making it more amenable for planting. Where damp conditions prevail, the soil becomes more open, allowing it to dry out better; if it is of a dry nature then the humus has the opposite effect, that of retaining soil moisture. All conifers love a humus-rich soil but not too much feeding with artificial fertilisers.

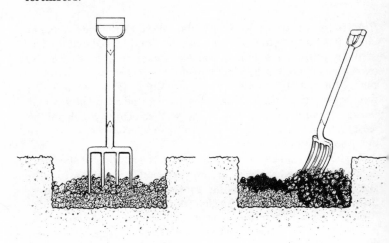

Preparing a bed for planting. Break up the subsoil (left) and then add humus and mix in (right).

Coarse sand will be a help when worked into the surface if the problem is a water-retaining soil. Where the site is wet, drainage will be the only answer for few conifers can cope with water at the roots, especially when newly planted. *Taxodium*, or as its familiar name Swamp cypress suggests, is the one conifer really at home in such conditions. Sometimes these trees can be seen with their feet actually in the water, although they will grow in normal soil too. As young plants they do not tolerate waterlogged ground as well as when they are older, so start them off on a mound of soil of sufficient height in order to ensure that the young roots are not immersed.

Position

Conifers of all groups normally demand a light position, well away from the competition of taller trees. Where planting needs to take place in shade, select from the green forms of *Taxus* or its allies as they tolerate these places better than most. Of the junipers *Juniperus × media* 'Pfitzerana' is possibly the best to have for the shade. No coloured foliage forms of any genera are really suited to positions other than in full sunlight. Planted in shade, their brightness is soon dulled to pale green. On sunless winter days, and in a garden where light is lacking, these golden types often start reverting to green, but they recover their brilliance when exposed to sunlight once again.

Hedges and screens

Preparation of the soil prior to planting should be most thorough. As permanent subjects the conifers will repay the effort over their many years of development. For a hedge, the ground should be trenched, breaking the sub-soil with a garden fork but not turning it over. Next spread some humus in the form of compost (garden variety), well-rotted manure, moist peat or leaf-mould in the base of the trench before turning in the top-spit again.

Do not confine the digging simply to the line of the proposed hedge for roots must be encouraged to spread outwards from what will become an evergreen canopy. This is almost as efficient as an umbrella in keeping the rain off the soil and because of this the sheltered area immediately beneath the branches tends to become dust dry in many soils. A wide-spreading root system will ensure that the roots do not suffer from lack of moisture for this reason.

Spacing depends on the species chosen. A single row of Leyland cypress can be put in 1 m (about 1 yd) apart down the centre of the dug area. Many Lawson cypress, *Thuja* or *Taxus*, should be closer than this, say 0·8 m (2½ ft).

Conifer hedges can be planted either in a single row (above)
or in a staggered double row (below).

When *Cupressus macrocarpa* are used to form a strong hedge they are frequently put in a double (staggered) row at 1-m centres (1 yd apart in two rows) with 0·5 m (1½ ft) between the rows. In a suitable soil they will meet up within three to four years and if

36

need be make a barrier against the worst sea-coast storms.

Do not forget to allow for lateral spread as well as height when deciding on a line for the hedge; of course, clipping will reduce this considerably when comparing a hedge plant with one that has developed naturally. The mature hedge must also receive plenty of light if it is to remain furnished to the ground.

Plant when the soil is moist without being waterlogged. Risk of total failure occurs when young conifers have to stand in water for several weeks after planting, and this can happen in some soils when the dormant season is chosen as the time for setting out. Whenever possible try to see that the soil is warm enough for new roots to form quickly; if the soil or air is dry a light overhead sprinkling with water will be much appreciated by the young plants. A little general fertiliser worked into the soil surface, a few days prior to planting out, will provide an incentive for the roots to travel and make establishment just that little bit quicker. Feeding should only be attempted on a very small scale for we do not wish to encourage too much soft top growth at the expense of root formation. This is especially so for the first season or two.

For hedging purposes small plants are to be preferred to specimens. Quite apart from the higher extra cost of established trees the smaller versions are more likely to grow away in an even manner. As young stock tends to transplant more readily, these would probably overtake the older plants in a few seasons anyway.

Individual trees, especially of such shallow rooters as Leyland cypress and *Cupressus macrocarpa*, when used for hedging, should each receive the support of a stake or bamboo for the first two or three seasons. Put in at planting time and see that it is strong enough to take the weight of a wind-blown plant. Alternatively, the transplants can be tied loosely to a strong wire stretched the length of the hedge line. The movement at soil level of an unsupported youngster is a great hindrance to it taking hold. Remove the stakes or ties when it is judged that the hedge has established a secure root system.

Nipping back of growing points by taking off about a third of the current season's wood has to be done in order to encourage bushiness. The season of planting will not be too soon for this to start. There is no hurry to get the garden shears out for a while as little in the way of regular trimming is required until individuals begin to meet up. Once started, an annual trimming will be needed in mid-summer when the growth for the season is slowing, and also a tidy up in the spring.

A wedge-shaped hedge, with a wide base, encourages better growth.

The best shape for a hedge is when the base is fairly wide with a gradual slope inward towards the top. Unlike a hedge in which the sides are perpendicular, this wedge shape allows light to reach each plant more easily resulting in better, more even growth. Once the plants begin to meet is also the time to decide whether or not to have a hedge, which will require trimming, or a screen.

For a screen, the conifers that started off as a hedge are thinned by removing every other plant leaving the remainder to grow on without trimming. Where a strong windbreak is wanted, several rows are planted with a stagger (alternate equal spacing in the rows).

Specimens

Specimen conifers that are to be displayed in grass are planted in prepared stations of at least 1 m (1 yd) in diameter. Dig out the top spit and place to one side. Break up the sub-soil, removing rocks or stones. Spread some humus source material in the bottom of the hole then backfill to the depth of the base of the conifer. Next, place the plant in position, staking first if deemed necessary. Complete the operation by filling in around the root-ball and firming as required. Keep the prepared area free of grass or weeds for several seasons until the specimen is maturing and able to compete. In wet sites the soil can be mounded slightly to allow the surface to drain. Where the ground is likely to be really dry, a saucer-shaped depression is suggested. This tends to retain any moisture.

Mulching the ground around conifers is most beneficial, for it helps to keep the soil moist and cool; it can be decorative too. For this use a thick layer of peat, screened garden compost, leaf-mould or shredded bark. We have even seen seashells used for this purpose. Before mulching see that the soil is moist and free from weeds.

Feeding

If anything, most conifers prefer a soil that is on the poor side rather than one rich in feeding. This is not to say that young plants do not respond or that it should be denied them. In the nursery area around Woking in England and Boskoop in the Netherlands, as well as elsewhere, there can be seen magnificent stocks of growing-on conifers of every kind in which feeding has played an important part in their development.

The soil is manured, often annually, and fertilisers added too. This is very often a fish meal or other organic compound. The aim is to establish an ideal fibrous root system which allows the plant to be lifted, transported, then replanted (often hundreds of miles away) without trouble. On poor soils, conifer roots tend to be sparse, growing long and coarse in their search for sustenance. For the garden plants a little added nutrient in the form of dried blood, hoof and horn, fish or bone meal will give a boost to growth with better foliage colour too. Just before the plants start to grow in the spring is the best time to apply feeding of this type. Just sprinkle it on the soil surface and very lightly hoe it in. Should the weather be dry at that time a gentle watering will ensure that it starts working right away. One must be more careful with the slow growing or alpine conifers for these are easily forced out of character if feeding is overdone. For these, a mulch of moist peat or shredded bark should suffice.

Planting

Purchased stock comes in a variety of forms. Some are bare-rooted from the open ground or perhaps have been grown in the soil then lifted with a root-ball that is kept intact with a piece of hessian (burlap) or polythene film. Others are pot-grown; formerly in clay pots, but these days more likely to be seen in metal or polythene containers.

Hedging conifers, Lawson cypress and thuja are frequently bare-rooted. This is satisfactory provided that the young plants have been lifted regularly or undercut to induce a fibrous root-system. If well rooted, there is no reason why these cheaper plants should not grow away well and develop into a fine hedge or screen. If the roots appear to be dry, soak them in a bucket of water for several minutes before planting out. The soil mark on the lower part of the stem indicates the former position in the ground of the growing plant – use it as a guide to the depth for replanting. Keep a damp sack ready to lay over the roots of plants waiting to be planted as the sun and a drying wind can cause irreparable damage if roots are left exposed. Do not worry if you are unable to plant right away due to unsuitable soil conditions. The young trees can be 'laid in' in a vacant plot until you are ready to deal with them. When planting, firm with the heel if the soil is moist or dry but with less pressure when wet. If really soggy, it will be better for the plants if the operation is delayed until soil conditions improve.

Bare-rooted conifers can only be put in when they are dormant. Using root-balled stock extends the planting season for a few weeks. In fact, if handled carefully, conifers lifted several months previously and kept with their roots plunged in moist peat can often be planted in mid-summer. Many materials used for wrapping roots, rot if left intact – others do not. The latter must be removed but *only after the plant is in its prepared station.* Pot-grown plants have a distinct advantage over the others that are normally sold as dormant stock, as they can be purchased for planting the year round. The purchaser also benefits by being able to select when convenient, then delay planting until conditions are suitable, perhaps weeks ahead. Losses of container-grown conifers are very few indeed if the advice of soaking pots (for several hours if dry) is heeded. Allow them to drain thoroughly before planting in the prepared site. In dry weather, it is also a good plan to water the soil the previous day in order that it too can drain by the time the plants are ready to go in. If, after the container is removed, it is seen that the roots in the pot base are very matted, these can be teased out carefully with a pointed stick. Do not break the root-ball or much of the object of growing the plant in a pot in the first place will be lost.

Containerised plants

Sometimes masquerading as container-grown are containerised plants. These have been produced in the open ground then placed in a container for selling purposes. This is not to say that there is anything wrong with the plants; in fact, they can be better than some old subject that has outgrown its pot. Yet it sometimes happens that, when removing the pot, all the compost falls away leaving a bare-rooted, open-ground plant. If it is consequently treated as such (after registering a complaint with the vendor!), watered, and kept shaded, there is every possibility that transplanting will be successful. These open-ground plants if purchased after they have re-established themselves in their containers compare very favourably with stock which has been container-grown throughout its life. Some conifers, notably junipers, do not make much root when grown in pots and care must always be taken to ensure that what little there is is kept intact when transferring from pot to soil.

Reducing losses

Most losses of recently planted stock are due to lack of water during their first season of growth. This applies to all transplants, especially evergreens and conifers. As well as maintaining a moist soil, they appreciate a gentle overhead spray now and then. Movement at root level was mentioned earlier as another cause of conifers failing to become established. This is remedied by staking the young plants. If lack of water is the chief killer of new stock, a close second is cold wind. To lessen its ravages, much good will be done by erecting a temporary screen of hessian canvas supported by stakes on the windward side. This can instead be a shelter of evergreen branches or hurdles which will assist the young conifer by reducing transpiration or water loss from the foliage caused by drying wind and/or sun. Special transplanting sprays, in which the leaves receive a coating of lacquer-like material, are much in vogue in some countries. We have not used these ourselves but feel that anything that can help a plant to get through this critical time must be considered an asset.

Selecting quality plants

What does one look for when selecting conifers from a garden centre or nursery? Whether growing in the open ground or in containers, the plants to choose are those which are young, vigorous, well-furnished stock, typical of the species or cultivar. 'Well-furnished' means that foliage should be carried well down, almost to soil level and with little trunk or stem visible.

There are some exceptions to this. In an immature cedar, for example, the stem will be seen although the other points apply. When, due to being grown too closely in the rows or kept in a pot too long, thuja or Lawson cypress have lost the foliage from the lower branches, this is seldom replaced. Such trees are best passed over in favour of younger stock which still carries plenty of foliage low down.

Where dwarf or slow-growing conifers are involved and there is a choice between large grafted plants and smaller specimens on their own roots, choose the latter for they will develop into plants more typical of the original form. Grafted stock will be recognised from the bump on the stem just above the soil mark. This is where the two halves of the plant have been brought together. When offered they are generally the only ones available due either to the difficulty in rooting the particular cv, or other economic reasons.

Where tall growers are concerned, such as the 'blue' spruces, *Picea pungens* cvs, cedars and the like, any worries over speed of growth will not apply. With these, try to ensure that it is a nicely balanced plant that is selected. This should have an evenly spaced branch system, together with, in the case of an upright grower, an erect, *undamaged* leader. This latter advice also applies to those species which have been raised from seed, for where the leading bud has been damaged in early life, two or

Beware of 'pot-bound' specimens, which will not grow well (if at all).

more replacement shoots appear with the result that you get either an uneven specimen or a tree with two trunks.

Now a warning about really pot-bound plants. On tipping the plant from its pot, a hard mass of tangled root is seen. Unless new roots can be coaxed from the hard ball which was once potting compost, little in the way of new growth can be expected. These plants are seldom satisfactory even when released from their pot prison.

Stock that has its origin in forestry nurseries seems to fall into two distinct categories. Young seedlings of forest conifers of two or three years old are excellent value providing that they have been transplanted. Older plants on the other hand are, generally speaking, not a good 'buy', for unless undercut they have remained unmoved for many seasons and instead of having fibrous roots theirs are coarse and stringy.

Nurseries are built on the reputation of the plants they sell. Most offer perfect quality although sometimes the choice seems rather restricted considering the range available. This applies especially to the alpine conifers. For these there are specialists who concentrate on nothing else.

4
Problems

The problems that affect the correct development, cause damage, or even the death, of conifers are varied. Some are avoidable from the outset; others can be corrected. Of those which are avoidable, the most common cause of failure is in transplanting. The so-called physiological disorders often come into this category too. They are largely overcome by the correct selection and placing of species to suit the soil and climate. A smaller loss comes about through fungus attack, and insect pests have also to be countered for they are not only responsible for the spread of some fungi but can themselves cause disfigurement.

Transplanting

Although the subject has been dealt with in Chapter 3, transplanting and the two or three seasons it takes for the plant to re-establish accounts for a possible 99 per cent of actual losses or partial failure. The most common problem here is water (either not enough or too much). Newly transplanted, the conifers are at their greatest risk from drying winds and hot sun. In exposed places, steps should be taken to prevent water loss through evaporation. Placing a temporary shelter made from hessian or plastic screening material around them will largely overcome the problem. If weather conditions permit, a fine spray of water can be given overhead in the evening.

On the other hand, too much water can be as bad or even worse than not enough. We have been called in to advise on a thuja hedge, newly planted in wet, sticky clay soil which was a virtual failure. Holes were simply dug in the soil which filled with water after the plants went in and the roots literally drowned through lack of air. If the planter had mounded the soil very slightly along the line of the hedge they would most probably have survived and done well.

Physiological disorders

Selecting the correct plants to suit the soil, climate and position will largely eliminate symptoms of physical disorders that may appear. It is obvious that losses of tender subjects will occur if they are planted in a climate that is too harsh for them. A late frost can also nip the shoots of a normally hardy form. If this happens after the new tips are showing these can shrivel and brown; sometimes new buds take a whole twelve months to develop from the leaders, with the result that no growth is made for the season. Trees usually make a good recovery when they grow away the following spring.

Chlorosis, yellowing of the foliage in a green plant, is most often the result of planting a calcifuge or lime-hating species in a soil containing an excess of lime. This comes back to correct selection again, for there are many which dislike alkaline (limy) soils. Saying this does not help anyone already owning a sickly plant because of this. Transplanting to a new position prepared with lime-free compost may be the answer where a dwarf plant is involved. Alternatively, an iron chelate such as Sequestrene can be watered in around the plant according to the maker's instructions. This will provide iron in a form that is readily taken up by the plant which should soon turn a healthy green again. Unfortunately, this is not a permanent cure and doses will have to be repeated at least twice each year.

Another cause of chlorosis is the too liberal application of fertiliser or fresh manure near the roots. Conifers do not, as a rule, show symptoms of other soil deficiencies.

Leaf scorch

Caused by wind, sun or frost, leaf scorch due to the lack of chlorophyll in the leaves is common especially on the white or yellow variegated forms. These have to be planted in the sun for their special feature to develop, so try to place these in a spot sheltered from wind where they get the early morning sun but remain out of its direct rays by midday.

Foliage scorch can also come about by splashing or contact with wood preservatives or their fumes, so be careful when treating a wooden fence if there is a hedge close by. Wind-blown weedkillers (especially the selective type) will also cause damage to tender growths. Once again, care must be taken to avoid this happening. Chemical sprays when used for pest control do not appear to harm conifers. If there is a choice, use wettable powder formulations avoiding any that are oil-based as the latter obscure the 'bloom' on the foliage and once covered this takes many months to reappear.

Diseases

Diseases of conifers are caused through fungal infection. Fungi are primitive forms of plant life often living in the soil and in or on plants. Many of these are beneficial to other plant life, and some conifers have a partial symbiotic relationship with a fungus in which the two rely on each other for their existence. Although many species of conifers (sometimes whole families) appear to be completely immune from disease, others are frequently victims of attack. In all cases, plants kept in good growth by attention to their cultural needs are less liable to succumb.

There are a great many diseases, and symptoms vary. These include discoloration or dropping of needles and leaves, rust-like patches on foliage and dead or dying branches. In most instances it is only practicable to treat young or dwarf trees. Spraying with a fungicide in spring and late summer (two applications at each time) will clear up minor attacks of most diseases. Others are more severe and will entail cutting away infected branches, which should then be burned. The wounds left must also be treated using an antiseptic paint. It is as well to use a sterilant on any cutting tools used to lessen the risk of spreading infection.

Where a tree has died as a result of disease and not just old age or drought, it too must be burned and the ground planted with a non-woody plant for four to five years before replacing a conifer in the same spot.

Insects

Some conifers are attacked by several insect pests which have to be killed before they cause unsightly damage to the plant and, by weakening it, allow the spread of fungal diseases. Spray with an insecticide two or three times at two-week intervals during the early spring and again in late summer – or at any other time the pests are spotted. As with diseases, it is the young plants which need this special attention in order for them to maintain their vigour.

As well as spraying against normal pests, galls which appear as swellings on the shoots of Norway spruce can be picked off by hand. These are colonies of tiny aphis which, if left, will stunt the tree. Caterpillars defoliating pine shoots can also be picked off where they can be reached, or a spray used for these too.

We have come across a combined aerosol pack which contains a fungicide and insecticide together. Although expensive this appears to be really effective, clearing up an attack of red spider mite on a specimen *Picea abies* 'Gregoryana' very quickly.

5
Growth Rate, Size and Shape

It is probably true to say that, for many, the ideal conifer would be one which quickly attained its desired size and shape and then maintained this more or less indefinitely without further growth. Woody plants such as conifers are not like animals (which grow until they mature and then remain the same size), but instead they continue developing until such time as their life span is coming to an end. Then growth finally ceases and a decline begins. Even many of the small 'alpine' sorts can become large in time, unless regular pruning, undercutting or transplanting is done. Where hedging and, more particularly, screening plants are concerned, we want the opposite; quick growth is the main reason for selecting certain kinds for this purpose.

In addition to the individual characteristics of each species or cv selected, there are other factors which govern the growth rate and affect the ultimate size of most conifers. These are: 1) soil; 2) situation; 3) climate. The latter can be easily seen where the same kind of plant is growing in different countries with varying climates. Under perfect conditions for the species, speed of growth and eventual height is frequently as much as double that of those plants which are growing in less suitable places.

Plants for rock or heather garden use should not exceed 2 m (6½ ft) in height or spread after ten years' growth. Moderate growers selected as isolated specimens can be expected to reach some 2-4 m (6½-13 ft) after a similar length of time, although this will depend largely on the size of the original specimen at planting time. The ultimately very tall trees normally commence life with a burst of speed, then slow down, and fill out over the years. For hedges and screens, planted in reasonable conditions, most suitable conifers will be well on the way to fulfilling their purpose after five years of growth.

Opposite: some typical conifer shapes. 1) Pyramidal. 2) Rounded bush. 3) Bun shape. 4) Prostrate. 5) Slender columnar. 6) Tall columnar. 7) Dwarf conical. 8) Broadly pyramidal. 9) Ovoid.

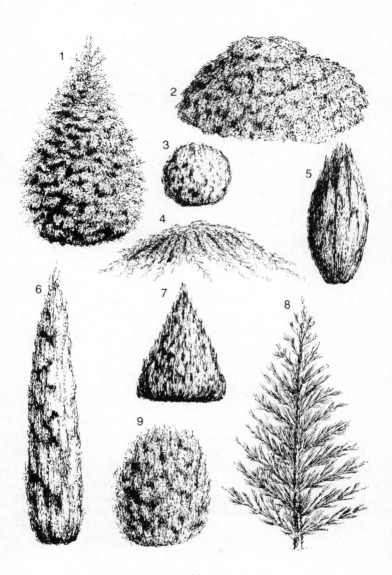

51

6
Descriptions of Useful Garden Conifers

This chapter is arranged taxonomically and for convenience the conifers have been divided firstly into families and then into genera and species. Subspecies, varieties and cultivars are described separately where they are of particular importance. Each description gives details of height, habit, climate preferences, cultivation tips, recognition features and uses in the garden. The common English name (where applicable) is given in brackets after the scientific name.

Ginkgoaceae – Ginkgo family

Ginkgo

This is a remarkable race of primeval plants of which but a single living species remains. Eventually growing 15-30 m (50-100 ft) in height, this is a hardy deciduous tree with unusual, un-conifer-like foliage. *Ginkgo* is not only of great botanical interest but also a highly decorative ornamental which thrives in a variety of soils, and being tolerant of atmospheric pollution is suitable for city gardens. Growth is upright, generally pyramidal; its undivided, fan-like, leathery leaves are green when in growth but change to clear yellow before they drop in the autumn. The sexes are on separate trees, and under ideal conditions the females bear crops of round green fruits which ripen yellow emitting a peculiar odour when they fall.

G. biloba (Maidenhair tree or ginkgo tree)

This is the single species from China where it has long been cultivated and no longer appears to be a wild plant.

Taxaceae – Yew family

Taxus

The yews are a small group of evergreen conifers with decorative foliage well-known for their ability to flourish on most soils either chalk or acid, provided that it is well drained. Apart from the golden foliage cvs, their garden usefulness is extended by their tolerance of shady positions in beds and borders. As they are able to withstand frequent clipping, another garden use is for hedging. The linear leaves are deep, shiny green in the species and, although spirally attached to the shoots, often arranged in two rows. Male and female flowers are normally on different trees and the cvs being clones are therefore either male or female. Male flowers are small, profuse, releasing clouds of pollen when disturbed. The females shortly after fertilisation develop into a nut-like seed which is carried on a green disc. The holder swells as the seed ripens to form a brightly coloured fleshy cup (aril). The seed is very poisonous to animals (including humans) and the foliage more or less so, for it is known to us to have killed horses yet has left sheep unharmed.

T. baccata (Common yew or English yew)

Growing to about 10m (33ft), this is a familiar small tree in the British Isles, where, as well as being one of only three native conifers, it has also been in cultivation since ancient times. The species has dark green, almost black foliage arranged in two rows on the side branches and radially on the leading shoots. A fine plant for hedging.

T.b. 'Fastigiata' (Irish yew)

This is the well-known columnar form, the erect branches bearing dark green-black leaves. Old specimens become wide-topped with several leaders.

Taxus baccata 'Semperaurea'. An eight-year-old plant,
75cm (30in) high and 50cm (20in) wide.

T.b. 'Fastigiata Aureomarginata' (Golden Irish yew)
Similar in outline to the above, but with clear yellow emerging
leaves which later become yellow or gold margined.

T.b. 'Repandens' (Spreading English yew)
A wide-growing plant with green foliage. With its downswept
branches, which have drooping tips, this makes an interesting
lawn specimen.

T.b. 'Semperaurea'
Dense bushy grower with very bright gold and cream foliage
retaining its colour well throughout the seasons.

T. cuspidata (Japanese yew)

A tree of moderate size in its natural habitat, but almost always only a shrubby bush in gardens. Slow growing and hardy, it differs from the more common English yew by its longer winter buds. The rather leathery leaves have a yellow reverse. Many cvs have been named in North America, where it is generally more hardy than the Common yew.

T.c. 'Nana'

Dense and wide-growing, this plant has thick branches with short shoots and radially arranged, dark green leaves.

Araucariaceae – Chile Pine family

Araucaria

These imposing trees are only found growing as wild plants in the southern hemisphere and all but one, the familiar Monkey-puzzle, are tender. Their growth is symmetrical with branches carried to the ground when young; older plants usually lose their lower branches as they age, developing into an upright tree with a well-rounded crown. The flowers of each sex are usually borne on different trees. The fertile cone breaking up when mature can be very large and contains edible seeds in most species.

A. araucana (Monkey-puzzle or Chile pine)

This tall, hardy tree with its stout trunk and long sweeping branches complete with dark green spine-tipped leaves is almost too familiar to need a detailed description. Planted extensively in Britain during a former era, its popularity is now on the decline in favour of smaller growing subjects. Quick-growing although rather tender when immature, the best specimens will be seen in country areas away from city fumes and dust.

Cupressaceae – Cypress family

Chamaecyparis

Formerly linked with *Cupressus* and often erroneously still listed as such, this important group of evergreen trees, although consisting of a few species only, has provided us with many favourite garden conifers. In most of the species the typical young plant is conical in outline, before filling out to become bell-shaped. In others, the foliage is not retained to ground level, so that one or several trunks will be formed. Seedlings commence life with soft, awl-like leaves before assuming their familiar flat branches, which are composed of tiny stem-clasping scale leaves.

Chamaecyparis lawsoniana 'Gimbornii'. A twenty-year-old specimen, 1m (3ft) high and 1m (3ft) wide.

Male and female flowers appear on the same tree and except for *C. nootkatensis* (which takes two years), most of the others ripen their cones in the first year. Providing that they have been shifted regularly all the members of this group transplant readily, even when quite large specimens. The many cvs exhibit the greatest variation from the wild plants both in colour of foliage and form.

C. lawsoniana (Lawson cypress)

A valuable timber tree of up to 60m (190ft), in North America
and increasingly used for forestry in Britain. The type forms a
tall stately specimen of green or greyish foliage, pyramidal or
columnar in outline with the leading shoots drooping at the tips.
Since the introduction of seeds from California and Oregon to
Lawsons Nursery, Edinburgh, Scotland in 1854, the flow of
numerous variants has been unending. They come in all shades:
green, yellow, silver, 'blue'; they are sometimes variegated; some
are tall and others dwarf. Because of the vast range of colours
and shapes, members of this tough, adaptable group have
become some of the more frequently planted conifers in Britain
and Europe. Although not very tolerant of salt-laden winds,
inland they are completely hardy. The best specimens are those
planted in moist soil where the climate is cool.

C.l. 'Allumii'
An old cv with grey-blue leaves still widely planted. The
branches are at first compact and upright but later becoming
more open as the tree gets taller.

C.l. 'Columnaris' syn 'Columnaris Glauca'
A superb plant which forms a narrow spire of bright blue foliage.
Useful where space is restricted.

C.l. 'Ellwoodii'
A well-known little conifer with grey-green juvenile foliage
which makes a fine choice as an upright subject for the rock
garden, tub or even lawn specimen. Although slow-growing,
unless trimmed lightly each year they will get surprisingly tall in
time. There are several mutations of this plant in cultivation
with the same dense, upright form. One of them ('Ellwoods
Gold') has pale silvery-green foliage overlaid with gold. This
becomes particularly bright in the winter.

C.l. 'Fletcherii'
This is a popular conifer of only moderate growth rate and
ultimate size. Although the semi-juvenile blue-green foliage can
be damaged by harsh winds, this is seldom noticed in normal

garden situations where the plant forms a dense pyramidal column usually with several leaders.

C.l. 'Gimbornii'

Almost globular in outline, this attractive garden conifer has dark green foliage marked with mauve at the tips. Slow-growing, it is suited for tub culture or may be used in the rock garden.

C.l. 'Gnome'

In the best form of this variable plant it is one of the slowest-growing of the conifers forming a ball of bright green foliage.

C.l. 'Green Hedger'

Selected as a seedling for its value as a hedging plant this is a dense, upright grower with bright green leaves.

C.l. 'Lanei' syn 'Lane'

This is a superb light golden yellow foliage plant, upright it will form a perfect specimen or a luxurious hedge.

C.l. 'Lutea'

The clear yellow foliage of this old cv, which is still frequently planted, is carried in feathery sprays. The tree eventually makes a broad-based column.

C.l. 'Minima Glauca'

This dense round bush very slowly attains about 1m (3ft 3in). The upright and side-ways facing fan-like sprays of deep green rather glaucous foliage radiate from the short trunk.

C.l. 'Silver Queen'

A broad-based pyramid made up of rather loose, spreading branchlets composed of pale green leaves so heavily overlaid with silver as to appear white. This tree is particularly attractive as it makes creamy-white new growth in early summer.

C.l. 'Stewartii'

Popular the world over this is an elegant, hardy tree with its yellow branchlets shading to green at their base.

C.l. 'Wisselii'

An upright tree of vigorous growth which really can be confused with no other. The greyish trunk bears sparse branches ending in clusters of dark green fern-like leaves.

C. nootkatensis (Nootka cypress or Yellow cypress)

Old trees of this species grow very tall in the wild with large trunks devoid of branches for several metres from the bole. In cultivation they are more often seen as slender pyramids and only filling out with age. The branches are spreading, green foliage slightly rough to the touch, the branchlets which are held more or less upright when young later become semi-pendulous with the tips drooping. They are very hardy and made good garden plants where a quick-growing, ultimately tall, tree is needed.

C.n. 'Lutea'

A fine, slow-growing coloured foliage form of the species, its golden leaves later turn to greenish yellow.

C.n. 'Pendula'

Spectacular as a young plant, this beautiful upright tree has spreading horizontal branches from which the pale green branchlets hang down curtain-like in two rows.

C. obtusa (Hinoki cypress)

A native of Japan and Taiwan this is a timber tree of some economic importance where, under forestry conditions, heights of up to 50m (160ft) may be attained. Trunks are straight, reddish-brown up to 6m (20ft) or more in girth. The foliage carried on crowded branchlets is dark green, paler on the reverse, thick and rather fleshy. The leaves are scale-like and blunt-ended (obtuse). Hinoki have long been cultivated in Japan as garden ornamentals. Several variations were imported into Europe and to Britain by plant-collector and nurseryman John Gould Veitch in 1861. There have been later importations since then. In spite of the fact that the species reaches a great height, the cultivars which we grow are either dwarf or in the medium size range, and all are suited to the average garden. The best results are obtained when they are planted in a moist, lime-free soil.

C.o. 'Crippsii'

Open in growth when young, this splendid form later develops into a small, sometimes broadly pyramidal, tree. The golden-yellow foliage is carried on elegant sprays which are spreading and have pendulous tips.

C.o. 'Kosteri'

One of the finest of the dwarf conifers this has thick, shining rich green leaves arranged in cupped sprays. They are frequently brown-tinged in cold weather to add to their attractiveness.

C.o. 'Nana'

Cultivated and almost revered by the Japanese for centuries this plant was introduced to the west about 1860. This now favourite the world over is a dwarf grower slowly developing into a rounded, flat-topped bush. The dark green leaves are also arranged in upwards facing cup-like sprays.

C.o. 'Nana Aurea'

A first-rate, slow-growing plant akin to the above but with clear golden leaves. It is more upright, however, and open, eventually forming a small pyramid.

C.o. 'Nana Gracilis'

This plant with slightly twisting, shell-shaped sprays of glossy green foliage is the best loved and most frequently seen representative of the group. It is a most accommodating plant with many uses in the garden: on the rockery, in the heather or pebble garden, or as a tub specimen (we have even noticed them used to form an attractive low hedge). The growth is slow, compact at first then broadly pyramidal.

C.o. 'Tetragona Aurea'

This highly ornamental variety was received from Japan in about 1870. A slow grower, but not really a dwarf unless growth is restricted by regular pruning. The upright, rather open, branch system is clad with flattened sprays which terminate in crested or moss-like glossy pale golden-yellow foliage, deep orange at the shoot ends during early spring. A protected site is needed for this one.

C. pisifera (Sawara cypress)

Introduced, together with some of its cultivars, from Japan first of all to the Netherlands in 1859 then two years later into Britain, this species has produced from sports and seedlings a variable range of garden forms, including some valuable dwarf plants. The wild tree is uncommon in cultivation, as it has attained a height of 20m (65ft) in Britain. Its cultivars are, however, popular. The species is conical in outline with a fairly wide base when young, slowly becoming a tree of graceful habit. Clad with shining green to tawny-yellow foliage, the level or somewhat pendulous branches sometimes layer themselves where they sweep the ground. Individual scaly leaves are rough to the touch and have a resinous scent when crushed. The foliage is carried on reddish shoots – a colour also apparent in the rough trunk. There are several distinct groups within the cultivated plants graded according to whether the leaves are juvenile, intermediate or adult.

C.p. 'Boulevard'

Introduced by an American firm this splendid plant has justly become one of the most popular of all garden conifers. Although eventually fairly tall – individuals of 6m (nearly 20ft) are on record – they are normally sold for use in the rock or heather garden, their height being regulated by frequent trimming. The soft, light blue-grey foliage is seen at its best when the plants are growing in acid soils of the cool greenhouse. In dry or wind exposed areas a partially-shaded site is to be preferred. They are not really suited to soils containing much lime, where the plants show their displeasure by changing to a dingy brown.

C.p. 'Filifera'

Growing into a wide-based bush or small tree this has long, spreading, pendulous branches with the whipcord-like branchlets carrying bright green leaves.

C.p. 'Filifera Aurea'

This is a smaller, slower-developing form of the above with clear yellow thread-like stems. Both make impressive 'landscape' trees for the smaller garden.

C.p. 'Plumosa Aurea Compacta'

A dense, compact, rounded bush and although upright generally more broad than tall. Foliage colour is light yellow, the leaves rather feathery and soft to the touch.

C.p. 'Plumosa Rogersii'

Dwarf and dense developing into a perfect cone of soft, bright yellow, juvenile leaves. This is a first-rate rock plant on account of its bright colour and neat manner of growth.

C.p. 'Squarrosa'

Pyramidal, the spreading branches have drooping tips. Dense, billowy, light blue-grey leaves are wholly juvenile and soft to the touch. Grown naturally, this forms a large bush or small tree in time but can be kept much smaller by regular trimming.

C. thyoides (White cypress)

A tree of pyramidal form occuring in the coastal regions of the south-eastern United States where it attains some 25m (80ft). The very few plants of the type species grown in Britain are relatively short-lived, seldom exceeding 10m. This is a very hardy species which grows naturally in swampy ground, not really thriving where much lime is present. The wild plants have fan-shaped branchlets bearing green or blue-green leaves.

C.t. 'Ericoides'

This bushy plant with soft, juvenile foliage undergoes a colour change each season when the blue-green of the summer growth turns to rich purple with violet shoots during the cold season. This is a splendid contrast when planted with other slow-growers, especially those with golden foliage. Slightly wind-sensitive in exposed gardens.

× *Cupressocyparis*

This is a small group of hybrids between *Chamaecyparis* and *Cupressus* that have come about naturally only in cultivation. Leyland cypress, the only hybrid to be extensively planted, first came to light at the beginning of this century, although it has only become generally popular in recent years.

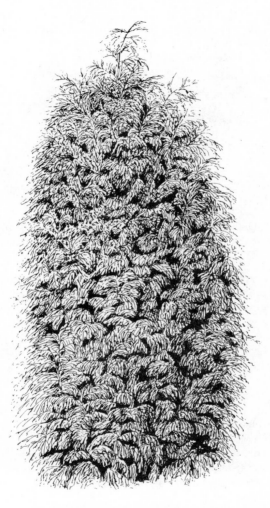

× *Cupressocyparis leylandii*. A ten-year-old tree,
7m (23ft) high and 1m (3ft) wide.

Cupressus macrocarpa 'Horizontalis Aurea'. A five-year-old plant, 1.5m (5ft) high and 75cm (30in) wide.

× *C. leylandii* (Leyland cypress)

These hybrids between *Cupressus macrocarpa* and *Chamaecyparis nootkatensis* are tall, spire-like trees with their foliage in flattened sprays similar to Nootka cypress but rather longer and more slender. The individual leaves are small and scale-like. Leyland cypress are of the greatest value for screening or tall hedges where a fast-growing evergreen is needed. The early plants were raised in North Wales; other clones have since come from Eire and near Wimborne, England.

× *C.l.* 'Castlewellan'

This is a now established favourite with its vigorous brown stems clad with light golden yellow foliage.

× *C.l.* 'Leighton Green'

The most frequently seen member of this group. It bears bright greyish-green leaves arranged in irregular sprays, thin at first becoming dense as the plant matures.

Cupressus

The cypresses are ornamental evergreen conifers, most of which have slender upright growth when immature becoming more open as they age. They are much valued in milder areas for screening, giving protection from sun and wind. The true cypresses are generally less hardy, especially when young, than the members of *Chamaecyparis* with which they are often linked. Protection from cold wind is therefore suggested until the plants are established. Adult foliage is minute, scale-like, pressed tightly to the stems; juvenile more open, feathery. The cones are relatively large, rounded, usually ripening in their second year but remaining on the tree for several seasons after the seed is shed.

C. glabra

This species develops into a pyramidal tree, its stout trunk covered with reddish bark with ascending branches with light silver-green foliage. It is a fine plant for a hot dry position and is reasonably hardy once established.

C.g. 'Pyramidalis'

Also sometimes called *C. arizonica* 'Conica', this quickly forms a spire of light blue foliage.

C. macrocarpa (Monterey cypress)

This, the most hardy of the cypresses, has a restricted distribution as a wild plant in Southern California, but is very common in cultivation. This is no doubt due to its usefulness for screening and is nowhere more valued than in mild coastal areas for filtering salt-laden winds. Growth is rapid, upright and pyramidal when young, often gaunt in old isolated specimens. The green rather thin adult foliage is only seen on these older plants which have been allowed to develop naturally. Clipped young stock tends to retain the juvenile soft form of leaf. Several golden seedlings have been raised and may be obtained as named cultivars.

Juniperus

Evergreen conifers of variable habit which ranges from

prostrate ground-hugging shrubs to large bushes and small trees. Some of the trees are large enough to be of timber yielding size. As the wild species occur mostly in the northern hemisphere they are almost all hardy in the British Isles and countries with similar climate although some may require a little protection until established. The aromatic leaves are awl- or needle-shaped when in their juvenile state and usually prickly. The adult foliage is scale-like and clasps the stems more tightly. Both forms of leaf frequently appear together on a plant, some (particularly the Common juniper) retaining more juvenile foliage, even when mature. Almost all of the junipers make good garden plants, especially where space tends to be limited and more naturally dwarf plants occur in this genus than any other. Also worth noting is the fact that several wild species choose to make their home on chalk or limestone and do well in similar soils in cultivation although it does not appear to be essential for their well-being. Any reasonably well-drained soil will suit them, either poor or fertile; the upright forms as specimens or in a mixed border, low growers on banks and rockeries. The two sexes of flower can be either carried on one tree or on separate individuals according to species. The cones or fruit look like berries and are really composed of fleshy scales; they often ripen in one year but sometimes take two.

J. chinensis (Chinese juniper)

A variable, generally tall species from China and Japan with upright, columnar or pyramidal form. The type, of which examples are seldom met with in gardens, has grey-green leaves, juvenile as well as adult appearing together – even on old trees.

J.c. 'Aurea' (Young's Golden Chinese juniper)

A very dense grower, conical in outline with clear yellow-gold foliage. Although eventually tall, it is slow enough to be used in most places with good effect.

J.c. 'Kaizuka' (Hollywood juniper)

An attractive plant with more or less upright branches and irregularly clustered branchlets of rich green leaves.

Interesting specimens can be formed by selective pruning.

J.c. 'Pyramidalis'

A fast-growing shrub of narrow conical shape. The juvenile leaves are glaucous green and very prickly. Like other plants of this group they require an open situation in which to develop best.

J. communis (Common juniper)

A hardy, variable species which is found over a wide range in the northern hemisphere. The foliage is wholly juvenile, awl-shaped, rather prickly. Male and female flowers are on separate plants, the latter bearing crops of blue-black berries from which, before they ripen, the flavouring for gin is extracted.

J.c. 'Compressa'

This extremely slow-growing tiny green column is a favourite for the smallest rock garden or scree.

J.c. 'Depressa Aurea'

A dwarf spreading plant with drooping, clear yellow new shoots. These change to old gold by the autumn and in really cold weather the whole plant assumes a purple-bronze hue.

J.c. 'Hibernica' (Irish juniper)

The familiar, dense, slender column of deep green foliage. These are suitable for formal situations where they develop their neat shape without trimming. They are also at home in the heather garden where the slim, upright shape breaks the flatness of the low mounds of the other planting. Cold windswept sites should be avoided.

J.c. 'Repanda'

Rapid growing dwarf carpeter suitable for using as fairly extensive ground cover. The dark greyish-green leaves, soft to handle, are carried on semi-prostrate brown stems.

J. conferta (Shore juniper)

This Japanese species is found growing wild in sandy sea-coast locations. Prostrate, dense growth with slightly ascending brown stems and large, soft, pale green, needle-like leaves.

J. davurica (Davurian juniper)

Widely distributed in northern Asia including Siberia the wild plant is no longer in cultivation. Some cultivars are however frequently planted.

J.d. 'Expansa Aureospicata'

A low spreading plant with very stiff branches bearing rich grey-green juvenile leaves with projecting stems of adult-type foliage. The whole plant is generously spotted with gold.

J. horizontalis (Creeping juniper)

A North American species, variable in the wild, all are low-growing, and most are prostrate. The branches are extremely long, branchlets are dense and usually short, the foliage is awl-shaped or scale-like, blue-grey in colour.

J.h. 'Bar Harbor'

Thin trailing leading shoots, side branchlets held upright. The grey-green leaves assume delightful mauve tones in cold weather.

J.h. 'Wiltonii'

This much-planted trailing shrub is at first completely prostrate; later the blue-grey stems mound slightly in the centre of the plant. This is the same as the cv 'Glauca' of the European nurseries and is invaluable where a dense low carpet of growth which smothers weeds with its strong outgrowing shoots is needed.

J. × *media* (van Melle's hybrid juniper)

These are a group of natural hybrids between *J. chinensis* and *J. sabina.* The individual members tend to fall into two groups, one more akin to the Chinese parent than the other. The important 'Pfitzerana' section are more savin-like with branches carrying a mixture of juvenile and adult foliage. The stems arch outwards from the centre of the short trunk to form a wide-spreading bush.

J.×m. 'Blaauw'

A most attractive plant originally imported from Japan. The thick, reddish, upright branches are heavily clustered with grey-green leaves together with thin projecting young shoots.

J. ×m. 'Hetzii' (Hetz juniper)

Where a large, fast-growing shrub is needed this will be a good choice. Bearing masses of light grey foliage it is adaptable to most types of soil and will also take heavy pruning by branch removal. Eventually large but can be contained easily.

J. ×m. 'Pfitzerana' (Pfitzer's juniper)

One of the most useful of all the conifers much valued for its quick growth and adapability. The long, densely-clothed branches of deep green foliage grow up and outwards before drooping at the ends carried down by the weight of the mass of foliage. The bush builds itself up layer upon layer as the years go by and where space permits it will eventually cover a wide area.

J. ×m. 'Pfitzerana Aurea' (Golden pfitzer)

At first a dense, low bush but later taller with the mature foliage glaucous green together with clear yellow new shoots. Very colourful and easy to grow.

J. ×m. 'Plumosa Aurea' (Gold-dust juniper)

This yellow version of the Chinese plume juniper ultimately gets too large for the rock garden where most seem to get planted. It is, however, a highly decorative form with upright, rather arching stems. The side shoots are crowded with pale gold leaves.

J. procumbens (Creeping juniper)

A vigorous spreading plant from Japan with stiff, prostrate branches of blue-green leaves which are arranged in threes on the branchlets. A useful mat-forming species valued for covering up bare soil.

J. sabina (Savin juniper)

This variable, long cultivated shrub from mountain areas of Europe and Asia has a spreading branch system with the stems more or less upright, clad with green or grey leaves. These are nearly all scale-like, adult in form, but the softer, awl-shaped juvenile type are also sometimes seen. All have a distinct odour when crushed in the hand.

J.s. 'Tamariscifolia' (Tamarix juniper)
This is a selected clone of the Spanish form of the Savin. It is extremely popular as a rock garden specimen and may also be used to good effect as ground cover or to edge a flight of steps. The prostrate branches clad with light blue leaves tend to build up layer upon layer until eventually a dense mat is formed.

J. scopulorum (Rocky Mountain juniper)

A small, narrowly pyramidal tree of western North America, usually seen with several trunks or stems springing from near the base. Branches are thick, branchlets slender with small scale-like leaves. Foliage colour varies both in the wild plant and in the many named sorts available.

J. squamata (Scaly juniper)

This is a variable plant in the wild, some are small trees, others low spreaders. The branches are generally stout, branchlets short, leaves large and carried thickly.

J.s. 'Meyeri'
Introduced to the west many years ago from a Chinese nursery garden, this now popular plant has large steel-blue leaves. It is normally seen as an upright shrub which will with training develop into an interesting small tree.

J. virginiana (Pencil cedar)

This hardy small tree is a native of North America, and as its common name implies the aromatic red wood has a commercial use in the manufacture of pencil casings. In cultivation, the plants seen are more bush-like with upright trunk, branches are at first ascending, and the branchlets are thin with small, sharp, scale-like adult leaves predominating with clusters of more open juvenile types here and there.

Juniperus virginiana 'Grey Owl'. An eight-year-old plant,
1m (3ft) high and 1.5m (5ft) wide.

J.v. 'Skyrocket'
All of the branches are strictly ascending on this, one of the
most exciting of all garden conifers to appear in recent years.
Their extremely narrow spires of silver-grey foliage are a
welcome addition to the garden, finding many uses both
formal and informal.

Thuja

This is a small group of evergreen shrubs and trees allied to, and
closely resembling, the flat-leaf cypresses from which they differ
chiefly in their egg-shaped cones with overlapping scales. The
foliage, aromatic if bruised, is scale-like in the species, but some
cvs retain the juvenile seedling type throughout their life.
Together with juvenile forms of other members of the Cypress
family, the latter were at one time accommodated in a genus of
their own called *Retinospora*, a name sometimes still seen in
catalogues. Their soil preference is for a well-drained moist site

where specimens develop into shapely plants, very dense, usually conical in form. The species as well as many of the cvs are fine hedging plants and in addition there are several slow-growing kinds suited to the rock garden. Male and female flowers are on different parts of the same tree, their cones containing a few seeds in each ripen late in the year. The common name originally given to *Thuja occidentalis* was Arbor-vitae. It means 'tree of life' and is seldom used except in books and catalogues, the Latin *Thuja* being preferred.

T. occidentalis (American Arbor-vitae)

Variable, usually very tall hardy tree from eastern North America with glossy green or pale yellowish-green foliage, usually changing to brown in cold weather. There are some fine garden forms including several dwarfs.

T.o. 'Holmstrup'

A narrow column of rich green, sometimes brown-tinged leaves held in tight vertical sprays. Although growing large in time it never becomes unmanageable.

T.o. 'Lutescens'

A dense, slow-growing pyramidal shrub of distinction. The new shoots and large flattened sprays of foliage are cream or pale yellow for their first season later becoming pale green within the plant.

T.o. 'Ohlendorffii'

Raised near Hamburg, Germany at the end of the nineteenth century, this unusual clone consists of grey, juvenile foliage arranged in four neat rows on the shoots with thin whipcord stems of scale-like adult leaves projecting from the ovoid bushlet. Annual (winter) removal of the latter is advised in order to maintain the neat appearance.

T.o. 'Rheingold'

A dwarf, broadly conical plant with a mixture of two types of leaves, the juvenile feathery sort present at the base of each branch which generally end in the flat adult sprays. The colour varies with the seasons from pale yellow with the young tips pink, later the whole plant becomes orange or rich old gold, particularly in winter when the bright colour is most welcome.

T. orientalis (Chinese Arbor-vitae or Biota)

A tree of moderate size from northern and western China which is frequently planted in its homeland and Japan. In the western world it is better known for the small, usually extremely neat, bush-like forms. The type species is sometimes seen growing as an old specimen. These have a short trunk, which has patches of shiny bark, bare upswept branches and a large domed crown of light green foliage held almost vertically, in flattened, yellowish-green sprays. For garden decoration the golden sorts are some of the best coloured conifers we have in the small to medium height range.

T.o. 'Aurea Nana' (Berkman's Arbor-vitae)

A first choice for many, this superb little plant develops into a fat, ovoid bushlet of dense upright foliage sprays, light yellow-green in colour.

T.o. 'Beverleyensis'

Dense, upright, eventually columnar in outline with its bright golden-yellow outer foliage tinged red-brown at the onset of winter wind and cold.

T.o. 'Rosedalis'

A dwarf grower with juvenile leaves and generally rounded habit. The foliage is soft to the touch and changes colour with the seasons, clear yellow new shoots mellowing to pale green then finally to grey-purple in the winter.

T. plicata syn *lobbii* (Western red cedar)

A very tall forest tree in western North America where the timber is highly valued for building uses. In gardens it develops into an elegant pyramidal tree with reddish-brown trunk and spongy bark; highly aromatic glossy green leaves clothe the spreading branches. The species, which succeeds best in a slightly moist, well-drained soil, withstands clipping well and for this reason is frequently utilised for hedging and screening.

T.p. 'Atrovirens'
This is a selected plant with particularly bright shining green leaves.

T.p. 'Rogersii'
A popular dwarf rock garden plant of dense conical form. The tiny leaves are golden yellow tipped with orange, bronzing in cold weather when it looks its best.

T.p. 'Zebrina'
An upright, broad pyramid in which the green leaves are clearly marked with zebra-like banding of gold and cream on the young growth. So heavy is this variegation that the tree could easily be mistaken for one of the golden cultivars when viewed from a distance.

Pinaceae – Pine family

Abies

The Silver firs are found in mountain areas of central and south-west Europe, Japan and North America. Some forty species are at present recognised, many of them of great economic importance and almost all eventually forming imposing specimens. Some of the wild plants are among the world's taller trees with individuals of over 100 m (more than 300 ft) on record. The best trees are those growing in deep moist soils in areas of high rainfall. Unfavourable conditions include shallow, dry, or (with some notable exceptions) chalky soils. Additionally some suffer from late spring frost – especially when young. The great height of many of the wild trees need not preclude the use of several species in the garden where growth tends to be more slow anyway. Their shape is symmetrical, conical in outline when young with a whorled tier of branches added annually. In the tall growers these lower branches eventually fall away leaving a straight, smooth trunk with branches radiating from the crown. The evergreen, frequently glaucous leaves are linear, almost flat with conspicuous white stomatic bands visible when viewed

74

Abies lasiocarpa 'Compacta'. A ten-year-old specimen, 75cm (30in) high and 30cm (12in) wide.

from below or when branches are lifted in a breeze. They are arranged in two different ways: on leading growths they are radially around the shoot, on side branchlets usually in two opposite ranks. Winter buds of leader shoots, their shape and whether resinous or not, the general appearance of the new growth and also cones are the means the expert has of distinguishing between the species, some of which were included with *Picea* at one time. The flowers appear in the spring with the numerous male flowers composed of a catkin-like cluster of red or yellow stamens carried on the sideshoots, the females nearer the tip. The upright clusters of fertile cones expand during the summer, some change from green to violet or yellow. In the autumn these all turn brown and break up while still on the tree almost as soon as they are ripe, with the seeds and scales falling together.

Cedrus

The cedars are a small group of distinctive evergreens well-known for the majestic ancient specimens to be seen in parks and large gardens. The value of their fragrant wood has been appreciated since early times and was formerly considered an important commodity of trade. Their tiny needle-like leaves are carried in two ways: spirally on the young leading shoots and in tufts on short spurs arranged on the mature branchlets. A slender pyramid when they are young the trees develop with a massive, often black trunk with wide, spreading branches. Their soil preference is for a well-drained sandy loam which remains moist during drought conditions. On mature trees the autumn-flowering male catkins are most prominent. No less conspicuous as they mature, either on the same tree or as separate individuals, are the large oval cones carried above the sweeping or upright branches. These ripen in two years, then break up while still on the tree. Some taxonomists have, in the past, regarded all the cedars as one species, individuals being simply geographical variations. They are certainly very similar and difficult to identify with accuracy when mature.

C. atlantica (Atlas cedar)

A familiar, eventually very large tree from the Atlas Mountain range in North Africa. The branches ascend strongly in a young plant but later they become more spreading, although almost always the pointed crown is retained.

C.a. 'Aurea' (Golden Atlas cedar)

Golden leaves shorter than the type. Pyramidal in outline, it is not as robust as the green sorts but in good soil will provide a satisfactory specimen.

C.a. 'Glauca' (Blue cedar)

With glaucous blue foliage the year-round, these are among the most popular of conifers for isolated specimens. A typical plant is large-growing with the upright branch system bearing white-blue needle-like leaves.

Cedrus deodara.

A ten-year-old tree, 4m (13ft) high and 3m (10ft) wide.

C. deodara (Deodar)

This eventually very tall Himalayan species is an elegant tree at any age. They are variable from seed and several named sorts are the result. All have pendulous branches clothed with light grey or grey-green needles some of which measure up to 5cm (2in) in length.

C.d. 'Aurea' (Golden deodar)

During the spring this splendid plant has golden yellow foliage on all exposed leaf surfaces. As the growth matures the colour becomes more greenish-yellow. Of value in the smaller garden not only for the colour but also for the slow rate of development and smaller ultimate size.

C. libani (Cedar of Lebanon)

This is the familiar cedar of our parks and larger gardens with massive black trunks and wide spreading branches. The young plants are pyramidal at first gradually becoming flat-topped with age.

Larix

The larches, one of the few genera of deciduous conifers, are of great value not only for the timber they produce but also for garden ornamentation. There are about ten species known, yet apart from those used in forestry few are in general cultivation; the less common kinds are seen only in arboreta or private collections. Most are rapid growing and, apart from the weeping cvs, conical when young. They form a straight trunk; old specimens usually lose their lower branches and form a wide, spreading crown. Carried on pendulous shoots, the needle-like young foliage – much like the cedars in form – is always a welcome sight as it heralds the spring, and the autumn colours of yellow or old gold are no less beautiful. In the garden their main use is for screening or planted in groups to form a shelter belt. They do well on most soils including poor sandy or gravel but dislike badly drained sites. Male and female flowers are on the same tree, the female catkins very showy when open on the bare twigs in spring. Their cones mature the first season and although the seeds are shed when ripe the empty cones remain on the twigs for some time afterwards.

Picea

The spruces are a large genus of evergreen trees often found in vast forests over much of the northern hemisphere. Many of these are valued for their timber and turpentine, a by-product. Young plants are normally pyramidal in outline with their branches arranged in tiers. Older specimens become, in some species, more open-branched with their trunks exposed. Their foliage is narrow, often hard, needle-like carried on small 'cushions' – tiny growths on the stems which remain after the leaves have gone which give the shoots a characteristic 'raspy' feel. Male flowers are in the form of round catkins, either red or yellow; fertile 'flowers' on the same tree develop into clusters of drooping cones which ripen in one season. When mature, these open to allow the winged seeds to drift away leaving the empty cones (complete with scales) on the tree to fall later. Several of the species are very ornamental garden plants, the large growers for specimens or screening; especially valued for smaller sites are the many dwarf and coloured-leaf kinds.

P. abies (Norway spruce)

This is a wild tree in central and northern Europe and also a familiar forest planted in Britain and elsewhere. These are Christmas trees in Britain. The shiny green leaves are carried densely on grey or reddish shoots. Cones are cylindrical, up to 15cm (6in) in length, carried in clusters. This species of spruce has, over the years, produced the greatest number of variations. Only a small number that have been named in the past are still offered by nurserymen.

P.a. 'Gregoryana'

A low grower which forms a dense mound of congested shoots which end in a mass of buds and long, spiny, dark green forward-facing needles.

79

Picea abies 'Nidiformis'. An eight-year-old plant,
30cm (12in) high and 20cm (8in) wide.

P.a. 'Nidiformis' (Nest spruce)
This leader-less variant of the Norway spruce develops into a
rounded shape with its short branches radiating from the
centre to leave a nest-like depression.

P. glauca (White spruce)

This tall, very hardy species comes from Canada and the north-
east of the USA where it is an important forest tree used for
milling. Of value for its hardiness and the ability to flourish in
bleak situations. The wild tree develops into the pyramid shape
typical of the group and is represented in cultivation by a most
attractive dwarf form.

P.g. 'Conica' syn var *albertiana* 'Conica'
This popular slow-growing form derived from the above
species is everyone's favourite for its neat cone shape and
bright green foliage. Originally found growing in the wild, this
can now be found in gardens around the world.

P. omorika (Serbian spruce)

There are few finer sights in the conifer world than a group of these slender trees rising spire-like from their surroundings. Of extremely narrow form, their pendant branches curve upwards at the ends. The leaves are bright green and silver; cones are small, conical, dark purple when immature. The species has a very limited range in Yugoslavia where they grow in acid accumulations among limestone rocks.

P. pungens (Colorado spruce or Blue spruce)

Specimens of over 30m (100ft) are recorded in the mountains of the western United States where the tree grows naturally. They are seldom seen as tall as this in gardens where the fine glaucous blue forms are more frequent. Because of their distinctive colouring named clones of these are among the most desirable of conifers in cultivation, suppliers often being hard put to meet the demand for established specimens. Their radially arranged leaves are curved and thick and the ends are prickly, carried on stout orange or white shoots. Bud scales are orange. Branches are in horizontal whorls, the tree developing into a broad-based pyramid when young, later having crowded branches towards the crown and a bare trunk. Thriving in dry soils the seed-raised stocks of glaucous forms as well as named cultivars are especially useful in their early stage of development with branches carried down to ground level.

P.p. 'Koster' (Koster's blue spruce)

An erect pyramid with slightly drooping branches, this is possibly the best known of the blue spruces. The tree's intense silvery-blue needles and neat shape make this a favourite for specimen planting.

Pinus

Occurring over most of the northern hemisphere, the pines are one of the best known ornamental and economically important groups of conifers. The many species range in height from low

Pinus leucodermis 'Compact Gem'. An eight-year-old specimen,
50cm (20in) high and 20cm (8in) wide.

bushes to tall trees. Because of their variability they are assured
a place in gardens large or small. Frequently conical in outline
when immature, trees normally develop a single trunk which is
invariably of attractive colour and form. The leaves are of two
types: small, papery, scale-like and deciduous appearing with the
new shoots; and the much more prominent evergreen needles.
The needles are usually in clusters of two to five joined together
in a sheath, six to eight in one species, or carried singly in some
sorts. These needles are almost always very dense on the
branchlets persisting for several seasons before falling. The
pollen-bearing male flowers are red or yellow; female flowers on
the same tree are woody and later develop into cones. After the

pollen has fallen on the open scales of the female flower these close, although complete fertilisation may not take place until almost a further year has elapsed. Once fertilised the cones grow rapidly to various sizes according to the species, normally ripening during their second year. Seeds are not always released when mature, some being retained within the cone for a good many seasons.

In addition to the quantities of millable timber produced annually from the pine, other products include rosin, turpentine and pitch from the resin; leaves yield commercial pine oil when distilled and the seeds are edible in many species.

A rather poor, well-drained acid soil suits them best, although in such a large genus of nearly one hundred species individuals can be found able to thrive in almost any soil and situation.

Pseudotsuga

The Douglas firs are a group of evergreen trees from North America, China and Japan, and although relatively few in species the Oregon Douglas is one of considerable economic importance. Except for its excellent but very rare dwarf forms, this species and most of the others are ultimately too large for many gardens – except that they are tolerant of a wide range of soils (excluding chalk), grow rapidly and have dense foliage so that they can be used to advantage to form a quick screen. The long narrow foliage suggests affinity to the Silver firs, being soft to the touch and fragrant when squeezed. The small pendulous cones mature in the first year and, after releasing their seeds, fall to the ground while still intact.

Sciadopitys

This genus contains a single unique tree of considerable garden interest. A very rare plant of central Japan where it is confined to two small areas, but also frequently planted in that country in parks and gardens. Old specimens in time grow into large, upright, usually single trunk trees although as they are slow growing they can be used in small gardens in spite of their eventual size. The foliage consists of two very distinct types of leaves: true leaves are small, yellowish-green, scale-like, appearing with the new growth. The more noticeable false leaves are cladodes, each composed of two needle-like leaves joined at their edges and appearing as one. Produced in whorls, they are deep shining green in a healthy specimen with a yellow line beneath. The whorled clusters of cladodes bear a marked resemblance to the ribs of an inverted umbrella which suggested the former name Parasol pine and today's – the Umbrella pine. Yellow male flowers are in small terminal bunches; females on the same tree develop into attractive, almost round cones which turn brown as they mature during their second year.

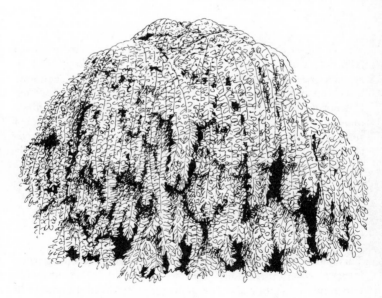

Tsuga canadensis 'Pendula'. An old specimen,
2m (6½ft) high and 4.5m (15ft) wide.

Tsuga

The Hemlock spruces are a race of evergreen trees with upright trunks, either single or multiple, and generally elegant drooping branches. Some species are fast growing in their native home and valued for the timber produced. *Tsugas* are also highly regarded garden plants, for where space permits the species develop into attractive specimens or an elegant screen. Among the many cvs of *T. canadensis* there are small growers available for the tiniest place. Where growing well there are few finer evergreen trees, the best developing in deep moist loam and showing a preference for acid rather than alkaline conditions. Their linear leaves, glossy green or glaucous with silver reverse, are thickly set, springing spirally from the shoot but usually appearing as if in two opposite rows. Unlike similar arrangements where the leaf tips lie parallel, in *Tsuga* they are uneven, for the individual leaves are unequal in length. Except for *T. mertensiana*, which has sessile, clustered cones, the mostly small cones are pendulous, ripening the first season but not releasing their winged seeds until the second.

Podocarpaceae – Podocarp family

Phyllocladus

An interesting group of conifers with unusual evergreen foliage. Almost all are native to New Zealand and Tasmania and only one, *P. alpinus,* can be considered hardy enough to plant outside in Britain. The plants of this genus have a completely different appearance from other conifers due to the fact that in the adult foliage stage the leaves are represented by cladodes or flattened leaf-like branchlets which function both as stem and leaf; the true or original leaves are tiny and scale-like. The flowers of each sex can be found either on a single tree or on individuals according to species. After fertilisation, the tiny nut-like seeds appear in clusters at the base of the growing shoots. Deep, rich soil is suggested in order to produce good specimens, but this applies to mild areas only.

Podocarpus

A large genus of mostly evergreen shrubs and trees. The few hardy species are variable in appearance, some slow growing and suitable for small gardens, others although eventually tall forest trees in their homeland are ornamental subjects when young; at least one species will make a good dense hedge. The foliage is thick, often hard and pointed, spirally arranged on the shoots. Flowers are normally present on separate plants. The colourful fruits are an added attraction when ripe with the single hard seed embedded in the end of a fleshy coloured stalk. Podocarps will grow in most soils including lime or chalk.

Taxodiaceae – Swamp Cypress family

Cryptomeria

A genus comprising a single, distinctive species. A native of Japan and China, it has also been planted in these countries since early times to provide a valuable source of timber. In deep, rich soil, well provided with moisture some very large specimens of over 50 m (150 ft) have been recorded. The type species when cultivated in Europe is rarely half of that height and small trees or large bushes are more usual. When choosing a site for planting, remember that a position sheltered from the cold wind will suit them best. As with most of the other evergreen conifers, the difference between juvenile and adult foliage is considerable; the former, open, awl-shaped and soft to touch, is retained in some cvs. Others carry a mixture of this and the smaller hard, adult type. A few are adult only. The foliage colour varies from the typical light green of the summer months to reddish-bronze or dull brown in autumn and winter. The flowers of the two sexes are carried on the same tree; males in terminal clusters, females on separate branchlets. Round cones are green at first and brown when ripe.

C. japonica (Japanese cedar)

This is the single species from Japan and China said to be

Cryptomeria japonica 'Globosa'. A ten-year-old plant,
75cm (30in) high and 75cm (30in) wide.

represented in cultivation by its var *sinensis*. A considerable
number of very fine cultivars have been raised and imported
from Japan in the past.

C.j. 'Elegans'

A popular, most attractive fixed juvenile foliage form, its
billowy masses of soft green leaves changing in colour as the
season advances, first to red then bronze during the cold days
of winter. An upright grower and eventually small tree.

C.j. 'Vilmoriniana'

Apart from another cultivar 'Compressa', this can be confused
with no other conifer. It grows into a tight, hard ball of dense
branchlets clad with tiny, recurved, light green leaves which
colour red when exposed to cold.

Metasequoia

This genus contains a single living species, which was discovered in Hupeh Province, China, as recently as 1941. Living specimens raised from collected seed were introduced a few years later. Like *Ginkgo,* these plants are also known as fossil remains and before the discovery of the living material they were thought to be long extinct. Deciduous, and recalling the Swamp cypress in form, this also shows an affinity for water, and the best specimens are seen where the soil remains moist in hot weather. The trunk, which in later life becomes deeply fissured, is covered in red-brown bark. Branches are upswept and form a pyramidal-shape. Foliage is fresh green changing to rust-red before being shed in the autumn. The cones are carried on the ends of long leafy stalks and ripen in their first season.

Sequoia

Tall, noble evergreen trees found in the wild only along the Pacific seaboard of the USA. The genus contains a single species which has among its numbers the world's tallest tree. Plants are narrowly pyramidal in outline with whorled branches, old trees retaining lower branches only when grown in isolation. Even here, much of the basal part is bare but usually with thickets of branchlets springing directly from the trunk. Under natural forest conditions they develop tall, straight trunks covered in thick reddish bark and often devoid of branches over much of their height. The dark green, abruptly pointed, linear leaves, recalling those of the yew, are in two rows on the side branchlets; on the leading shoots they are smaller, radial, clasping the stem. Damage to leaves by frost and wind does not appear to restrict growth although it is unsightly and is a point to be borne in mind when selecting a site for the two splendid cvs mentioned below. The flowers of the two sexes are on the same tree, the females forming small rounded cones which ripen in two seasons and remain on the tree for several years.

Sequoiadendron

Giant trees allied to *Sequoia*, from which they differ mainly in their scale-like leaves. They do not attain such great height as the other redwood or large Douglas firs, but are massive in girth and live to a great age. Some of the specimens seen in Britain (where they are planted in parks and large gardens, or perhaps as an avenue leading to a great mansion) are the original seedlings sent out by the nursery firm of Veitch of Exeter. These seedlings were raised from seed obtained by their collector William Lobb in 1853. Individual leaves are tiny, carried thickly on slender shoots which hang in great bunches on the side branches. The red-brown bark is a feature on trees of all ages; it gets extremely thick in time and can be punched hard without hurting the fist. Cones, larger than those of *Sequoia*, ripen in their second year.

Taxodium

Hardy, tall, deciduous trees with attractive foliage from the USA and Mexico. Apart from very dry soils (which are best avoided) they thrive in most sites, including really wet places such as pond sides. The tree comes into leaf very late in Britain – one of the last to do so. The leaves have a delicate feathery appearance, pale green at first. Shoots are of two kinds: the leading shoots in which the leaves grow spirally are retained, and the side branchlets where the leaves are carried in opposite rows are deciduous, falling with the now rust-red leaves in the autumn. The round cones are carried on short stalks and ripen the first season.

Select Bibliography

Bean, W. J., *Trees and Shrubs Hardy in the British Isles*, Vols. 1-4, 8th edition, John Murray 1970-80

Harrison, C. R., *Ornamental Conifers*, David and Charles 1975

Hillier, H. G., *Manual of Trees and Shrubs*, 5th edition, David and Charles 1981

Mitchell, A., *Trees of Britain and Northern Europe*, Collins 1974

den Ouden, P., and Boom, B. K., *Manual of Cultivated Conifers*, Nijhoff, The Hague 1978

Glossary

ACID (soil) Lime-free.

ALKALINE (soil) Containing lime or chalk.

APEX OR APICE (plural) Topmost.

APICAL BUDS *see* Apex.

ASCENDING Curving upwards.

ARIL Fleshy seed holder.

AWL-LIKE A leaf, often slightly curved, tapering from the base to the tip.

AXIL The angle between branch and branchlet or branchlet and leaf.

BREAK To branch; to send out new shoots from dormant wood.

COLUMNAR Narrow cylindrical, column-like.

COMPOST Mixture of prepared soils used for potting, *see also* Garden compost.

CONE Seed-bearing structure.

CONELET Immature cone.

CONICAL Cone-shaped.

CULTIVAR An internationally accepted term for a plant only found in cultivation.

DECIDUOUS Losing leaves in one season or less.

ELITE Specimens selected for excellence.

EVERGREEN Leaves retained the year-round.

FASTIGIATE Branches upright close together.

FERTILE FLOWER Seed-bearing.

GARDEN COMPOST Correctly rotted down garden refuse.

GLAUCOUS Foliage with a covering of 'bloom', usually grey or bluish.

HUMUS Powder-like particles in the soil derived from decayed vegetable matter.

LATERAL Emerging from the side.

NODE Leaf joint; in cònifers often the division between two years' growth.

PENDULOUS Drooping downwards.

PLUMOSE Feathery.

PROSTRATE Lying flat on the ground.

PYRAMIDAL Broad-based tapering evenly towards the tip.

SCALE A minute form of leaf, often adult, sometimes papery and deciduous.

SPORT Bud mutation, frequently the source of a new cv.

SPUR Short, stiff branchlet.

STOMATIC Bands of 'breathing pores' (stoma) on the foliage, usually grey or white.

STRIKE To root.

STROBULUS Cone- or catkin-like arrangement of male and female flowers.

TYPE The original specimen to be named, but usually taken to mean the normal form of a plant.

Index

Figures in *italics* refer to page numbers of illustrations.

Abies 12, 74-5
  Lasiocarpa 75
Angiospermae 11
Aphis 48
Araucaria 12, 55
  araucana 31, 55
Arbor-vitae 72
  American 72
  Berkman's 73
  Chinese 73

Background groups 31-2, *32*
Balsam 7
Bare-rooted plants 40-1
Belon, Pierre 7
Biota 73

Caterpillars 48
Cedars 76-8
  Atlas 76
  Blue 76
  Golden Atlas 76
  Japanese 86
  of Lebanon 78
  Pencil 70
  Western red 23, 73
Cedrus 76-8
  atlantica 76
  deodara 77, 78
  libani 78
Chamaecyparis 24, 28, 55-62
  lawsoniana 17, 22, *56*, 57-8

  nootkatensis 23, 56, 59, 64
  obtusa 59-60
  pisifera 19, 22, 60-2
  thyoides 62
Chile pines 55
Chlorosis 46-7
Classification 11-19
Climate 49
Clipping 37
Clones 18-19
Colour 20-1
Compost 34, 35
Cone 7, *9*
Coniferae 11
Containerised plants 41-2
Cryptomeria 86-7
  japonica 86-7, *86*
Cultivars 17-19
Cultivation 33-44
Cupressaceae 55-74
× *Cupressocyparis* 62-4
  leylandii 63, 64
  macrocarpa 64
Cupressus 62, 64-5
  arizonica 65
  glabra 24, 65
  lusitanica 24
  macrocarpa 22, 36, 37, 65
  sempervirens 24
Cypresses 33, 55-74
  Dawn 33
  Hinoki 59

Lawson 27, 28, 36, 40, 57-8
Leyland 36, 37
Monterey 22, 65
Nootka 59
Sawara 60-2
Swamp 33, 34, 86-9
White 62
Yellow 59

De Arboribus Coniferi 7
Deciduous conifers 21
Deodar *77*, 78
  Golden 78
Dioecious plants 11
Diseases 47-8
Dwarf conifers 26

Engler 11
Evergreens 20

Families 14-15
Feeding 37, 39-40
Fertilisers 39
Firs
  Douglas 8
  Silver 33
Foliage 12, *12*, 13
  juvenile 13
Forms 14-15
Foundation planting 27-8, 30
Framing the garden 21-3
Fungal infection 47-8
Fungicides 48

Galls 48
Genera 14-15
Ginkgo 52-3
  biloba 53
Ginkgoaceae 52-3
Ginkgos 21, 52-3
Grafted stock 43
Ground cover 26-7
Growth rate 49-50
Gymnospermae 11

Heather gardens 24-6
Hedges 22, *22*, 35-8, *36*, *38*
Humus 34, *34*, 35
Hybrids 16-17

Insect pests 48
Insecticides 48

International Code of Botanical
  Nomenclature 14

Junipers 7, 23, 33, 42, 65-71
  Chinese 66
  Common 67
  Creeping 68, 69
  Davurian 68
  Gold-dust 69
  Golden Chinese 66
  Golden Pfitzer 69
  Hetz 69
  Hollywood 66
  Irish 67
  Pfitzer's 69
  Rocky Mountain 70
  Savin 69
  Scaly 70
  Shore 67
  Tamarix 70
  van Melle's Hybrid 68
Juniperus 27, 65-71
  chinensis 17, 66-7
  communis 24, 25, 26, 29, 67
  conferta 67
  davurica 68
  horizontalis 26, 68
  × *media* 35, 68-9
  procumbens 8, 69
  sabina 26, 69-70
  scopulorum 70
  squamata 70
  virginiana 70-1, *71*

Landscape design 30-1
Larix 78-9
Leaf-mould 34, 35
Leaf scorch 47
Linnaeus 13
Losses 42

Maidenhair tree 53
Manure 34, 35
Metasequoia 88
Monkey-puzzle 31, 55
Monoecious plants 11
Mulching 39

Noah's Ark tree 25

Ornamental Gardening 8

Papworth 8
Peat 34, 35
Phyllocladus 85
Physiological disorders 46-7
Picea 79-81
  abies 17, 79-80, *80*
  glauca 25, 80
  omorika 81
  pungens 23, 43, 81
  sitchensis 9, 33
Pinaceae 74-85
Pines 33, 74-85
  Scots 21
Pinus 12, 81-3
  leucodermis 82
  mugo 33
  nigra 33
  sylvestris 9, 33
Planting *34*, 35, 40-1
Podocarpaceae 85-6
Podocarps 85-6
Podocarpus 86
Position 35
Pot-bound plants *43*, 44
Pot-grown plants 40-1
Pseudotsuga 83

Red spider mite 48
Redwoods, Coast 8
Resin 7
Rock gardens 24-6, *25*
Root-ball 40, 41
'Rule of Priority' 14

Sciadopitys 83-4
Screens 22, 35-8
Selection of plants 42-3
Sequoia 88, 89
  sempervirens 8, 17
Sequoiadendron 89
  giganteum 8
Shape 49-50, *51*
Situation 49
Size 49-50, *51*
Soil 33-5, 49
  preparation 34-5
  types 33
Spacing 36
Species 14-15
Species Plantarum 13
Specimens 39

Spruces 33
  Blue 81
  Colorado 81
  Koster's blue 81
  Nest 80
  Norway 23, 79
  Serbian 81
  Sitka 33
  Western hemlock 23
  White 80
Subspecies 15-16
Synonyms 15

Taxaceae 53-5
Taxodiaceae 86-9
Taxodium 33, 34, 89
Taxonomy 14
Taxus 22, 33, 35, 36, 53-5
  baccata 17, 27, 53-4
  cuspidata 54-5
Thuja 22, 24, 28, 33, 36, 71-4
  lobbii 73-4
  occidentalis 18, 23, 72-3
  orientalis 73
  plicata 29, 73-4
Thujopsis 33
Transplanting 45-6
Trimming 38
Trough gardens *29*, 29
Tsuga 33, 84-5
  canadensis 84, 85
  heterophylla 9, 23
  mertensiana 85
Tubs 28, *28*

Varieties 15-16
von Linné, Carl 13

Water 45-6
Wellingtonia 21
Windbreaks 22, *22*, 38

Yews 7, 53-5
  Common 53
  English 53
  Florence Court 27
  Golden Irish 53
  Irish 27, 53
  Japanese 54
  Spreading English 54